GARDEN ROUTE GUIDE

FROM STILL BAY TO STORMS RIVER

False Plum Anemone
Pseudactinia flagellifera

JACANA**MAPS**
The Right Direction

Acknowledgements

We would particularly like to thank Val Thomas for her dedication, passion and energy without which this Eco-Guide series would not have been possible.

As part of this series, the Garden Route Guide is a beautifully illustrated and integrated book about this fascinating coastal area. The creation of this book has been a journey of discovery, and has involved the expertise and hard work of many people. The support of both South African National Parks, Western Cape Nature Conservation Board and Dr Izak Rust is particularly appreciated. Jacana would like to acknowledge the following individuals and organisations for their commitment and contribution to making this book a reality.

Text Development and References
Dr Izak Rust (Koringberg Toere, Franschhoek); Dr Roy Lubke and Dr T. Avis (Dept. of Botany, Rhodes University); SOEKOR; Morné van Zyl; Avril Craig; Clare Archer (National Botanical Institute); Tom Barry (Gamka Mountain Nature Reserve); Ken Coetzee (Conservation Management Services); Andrew West, Mike Brett and Anne Lise Vlok (Western Cape Nature Conservation Board); Greg Vogt (S.A. Whale Watching); Jan Vlok (Regalis Environmental Services); Dave Edge and the Knysna Lepidoptery Society; Glynis Clacherty (Clacherty and Associates); Morné Bezuidenhout (University of Port Elizabeth); Dr B. Branch, Dr V.G. Cockcroft, Dr Norbert Klages and Dr Malcolm Smale (Port Elizabeth Museum); June and Peter Cattell (Goukamma Nature Reserve); Mrs F. Saayman (Department of Constitutional Planning and Development); Dr Warwick Sauer (Sea Fisheries Research Institute); Gary van der Merwe; Els Dorrat; Anthea Rousseau; Judith Hopley; Dave Gear; Linda Paxton; Shantal Bulbring; Jean Boonzaier; Lynne Broomhall; Norman Elwell (The Lakes Bird Club); Jim Hallinan (S.A. National Parks); Rob Erasmus (Enviro Divers); Prof. G. Marsh (Rhodes University); Jacana Team

Photographs and Photographic Reference
Gary van der Merwe; Gerhard Dreyer; Lance van Horsten; Marty Reddering; Western Cape Nature Conservation Board; Kelvin Saunders; Lisl Barry; Roger de la Harpe; Nigel Dennis; Clive Webber; Jacana Team. With acknowledgements to the Waves B & B and George Museum for the history introduction photograph

Garden Route Maps
Lourens du Plessis, MetroGIS
Original Map Development: Automobile Association of South Africa; Rodger Smith (Eastern Cape Nature Conservation); Willie Brink (SAFCOL); Theo Stehle and Cobrie Vermeulen (Department of Water Affairs and Forestry); Gary van der Merwe; Gwen Haynes; Jacana Team

Text and Artwork Evaluation
Johan Fourie (National Parks Board); Ken Coetzee and Andrew West (Cape Nature Conservation); Tertius Carinus (Tsitsikamma National Park); Dr P.C. Heemstra, Prof C. McQuade, Dr A.K. Whitfield (Rhodes University); Dr Shaleen Els (University of Port Elizabeth); Prof. Cannone (Dept. of Biology, Wits University); Jeff Lockwood (Bird Life South Africa); Dr Janette Deacon; Glynis Clacherty (Clacherty and Associates); Marius Burger (Sungazer Adventures); Jacana Team

Design and DTP Origination
Jacana Team

CONTENTS

Bottlenosed Dolphin,
page 41

THE GARDEN ROUTE –
LAND AND SEA

The "Garden Route" was conceived over 50 years ago to promote the diverse and beautiful coastal plain that lies between the Outeniqua and Tsitsikamma mountains on the north, and the Indian Ocean on the south.

The "Garden" varies greatly as the magic of the 140 kilometre Route unfolds. Low in height, but dense in species, pristine fynbos dunes and cliffs merge with towering indigenous forests. A few gentle rivers meander on lower plains, while many easterly rivers cut massive, steep-sided gorges through the spectacular mountains. Plunging shoreline cliffs interspace with soft, sandy beaches in half-heart bays, linked by boulders and pebbles thrown up by the strength of the ocean over millennia. Yes, there is also urbanisation and industry, to add the human backbone and facilities, that all add up to making this a holiday paradise for anyone who enjoys the outdoors.

A peaceful gorge-side along the Otter Trail showing Table Mountain quartzite.

SETTING THE SCENE

The "Garden Route" area is a microcosm of any of the Earth's major coastal areas – sea shore, dunes, cliffs, rivers, gorges, estuaries, lakes and mountains.

The rock layers of the Earth's crust change with time. Mountain peaks and river gorges are formed by weathering and erosion, while landforms, such as dunes, are the result of sedimentation.

Weathering – rock is broken down into smaller pieces by ice, water, heat, rivers, glaciers, surf, the effect of plant roots and chemical reactions.

Rock formation – the sediment is subjected to millions of years of cementing, pressure, heat, and often crustal upheaval. This gradually forms new rock with new characteristics.

Erosion – this is when weathered material is transported by water, wind, river, waves, ice or gravity.

Sedimentation – eroded material is eventually deposited, often in layers, in a new place.

Earth Structure
1. Metallic core
2. Very hot mantle
3. Thin crust

Earth Structure
The Earth is a sphere with a red hot metallic core, surrounded by a mantle of very hot, soft and supple rock. We live on the very thin, cool crust of the surface.

Crustal Plates
The crust is made up of many different-sized plates which are floating on the very hot mantle. They move very slowly, up to 15 cm per year. There are eight larger plates shown here. When two plates collide, their edges crumple and fold, and this has monumental implications.

This is how continents are created, or split apart, how mountains are bulldozed upwards, and how vast new oceans flood in between two landmasses. These plates are still moving, and the world map as we know it today will be noticeably different in a million years time.

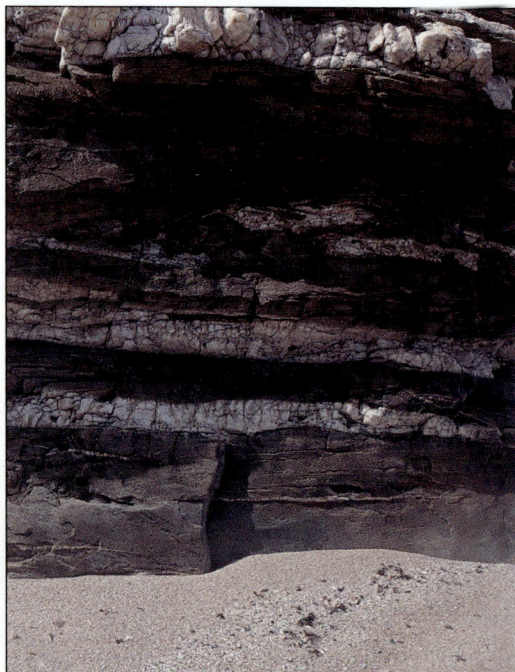

If the earth were the size of an apple, the crust would be thinner than the apple's skin.

Close up of quartzite rock showing weathering from rock to sand.

Crustal Plates
1. Pacific Plate
2. Nazca Plate
3. North American Plate
4. South American Plate
5. African Plate
6. Asian Plate
7. Antarctic Plate
8. Indo-Australian Plate

4

Gondwana super-continent 400 million years ago (Ma)

Every few hundred million years some of the crustal plates collide and form super-continents. About 400 million years ago (Ma), the area we call the Garden Route, lay under an inland sea on the giant super-continent Gondwana.

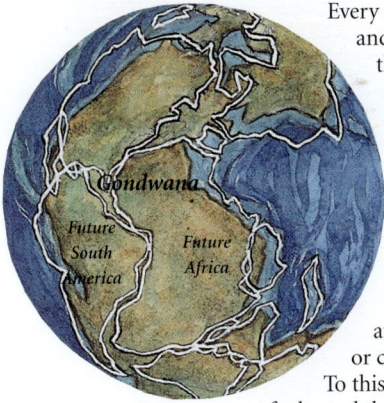

Sediment was washed into this sea by rivers flowing from present-day Namaqualand. This was deposited in layers on a granite base. The sediment was pressurised, heated and turned into very hard rock – Table Mountain quartzite (TMQ). This is distinguished by cracks, faults and weaknesses between layers of the ancient sediments. Many of these intersect each other at acute angles, or close to 90º. To this day these faults and the cracks are visible (map page 6).

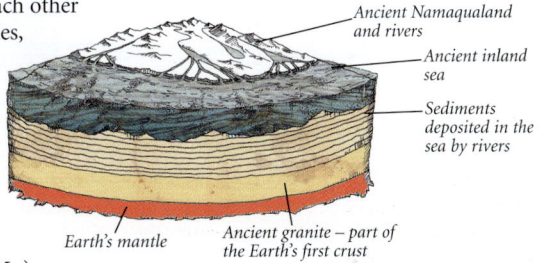

Ancient Namaqualand and rivers

Ancient inland sea

Sediments deposited in the sea by rivers

Earth's mantle

Ancient granite – part of the Earth's first crust

The Rise of the Cape Fold Belt Mountains (260 - 230 Ma)

Cape Fold Belt Mountains

The Garden Route shares major features with the southern Cape – the Indian Ocean coastline to the south, and the Cape Fold Belt Mountains to the north.

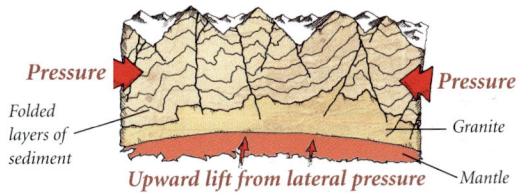

About 260 Ma, crustal plate collision led to the final formation of Gondwana. The huge pressure folded, crumpled and tilted the horizontal layers of the sediment and rock, and pushed them upwards. This created a mighty mountain range, thousands of metres high called the Cape Fold Belt Mountains. These mountains include the Outeniquas and the Tsitsikammas.

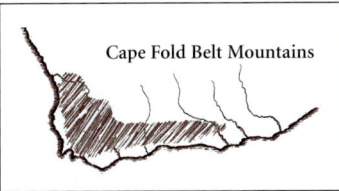

Pressure

Pressure

Folded layers of sediment

Granite

Upward lift from lateral pressure

Mantle

Pinch the skin on the back of your hand to see this effect.

Erosion along many rivers reveals the layers and folding of Table Mountain quartzite.

SETTING THE SCENE

COASTLINE AND SEA LEVEL CHANGES

Of all the planets in our Solar System, Earth is the only one with water and coastlines. The fascinating line where sea meets land is surprisingly unstable. Any major change to the Earth's crust, or to the amount of water in the oceans, profoundly affects the position and shape of coastlines. This in turn alters erosion, sedimentation, rock formation and weather cycles.

Beach stones sculptured by time and the elements, to reveal their intriguing shapes and patterns.

The Indian Ocean Coastline forms (Cretaceous Period – 140 Ma)

From 140 Ma during the Cretaceous period and the breakup of Gondwana into the continental masses of the southern hemisphere, new oceans were progressively formed. The Garden Route coastline formed while the southern tip of South America and the Falkland Islands (wrapped around the southern part of Africa) moved westwards away from Africa. This allowed the new Indian Ocean to encroach from the east. This new coastline was the start of the Garden Route landscape as we see it today.

Both before and after these events, sea level changed many times (see opposite). During times of higher water-level than today, rivers washed sand and mud into the Cretaceous bays around Plettenberg Bay, Knysna and Mossel Bay.

These Cretaceous mud and sand sediments settled, but were never pressurised and heated to the same extent as the TMQ. The resulting Cretaceous mudstone and sandstone are not nearly as tough, and they weather relatively easily. They do not show the acute 90° angle cracks that characterise TMQ.

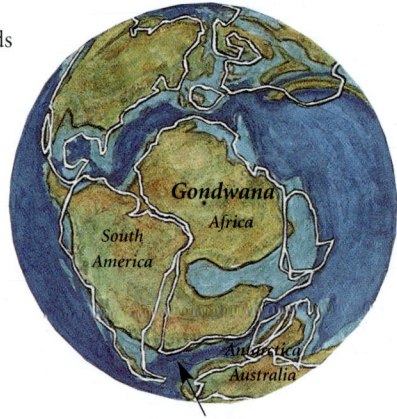

Indian Ocean forming

Simplified Geology

Mostly sand / sandstone / limestone / fossil dune sand deposited 15 Ma and younger

Cretaceous mudstone deposited about 120 Ma

Table Mountain quartzite (TMQ) deposited about 450 Ma, folded about 260 Ma

George granite deposited about 620 Ma

All the above have associated rocks. For simplicity these have not been included.

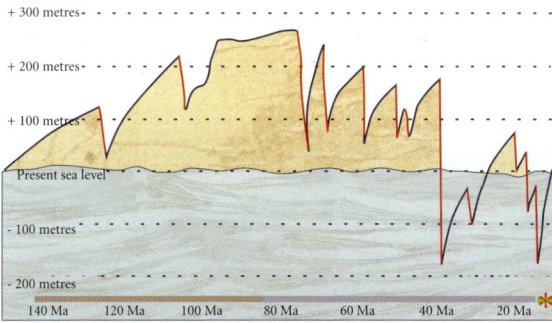

Changes in global sea level from 140 Ma to the present

Fluctuations in sea level   ~ Rivers cut the gorges
— Cretaceous Period   Tertiary Period   ✳ Present Day

Sea Level Changes (140 Ma to present time)

During the last 140 million years, the sea level along the Garden Route has changed frequently. Sea level changes can result from the global variation of sea level and from more local tectonic effects that cause the land to rise or sink relative to the ocean. In the past, sea level changes of up to 300 m above and 200 m below present level have occurred. Those sea level changes have profoundly affected the near coastal zone along the Garden Route.

Archeological evidence at Nelson Bay Cave at Robberg is clearly displayed for visitors. This cave was used by hunter-gatherers and herders some 18 000 years ago as a shelter (see site 31 on pages 125 & 126). Layers of their domestic refuse (middens) show that their diet changed from sea products, like shellfish, to land animal sources only, and then back to fish again.

Proof of sea level changes are aided by early humans' utilisation of sea food such as these shells, found in middens (page 106).

These diet changes occurred because the sea level fell by some 100 metres, and the shoreline receded to a point many kilometres away from the cave. At this time their diet was predominantly meat, because they could not walk to the sea and back in one day. Significant sea level changes are therefore not unusual, and more changes can be expected. Present changes in global climate indicate that a rise in sea level of up to one metre in the next 100 years is likely. If this should happen, the coast could move inland as much as 3 - 5 kilometres in some low-lying areas. Estuaries such as the Keurbooms, Piesang, Knysna (to right) and Kaffirkuils would certainly be flooded. At 300 metres higher, the sea would flow over all the bridges of the gorges and over the entire town of George, right up the Gourits, Piesang, Knysna and Keurbooms River valleys. Olifantsberg (357 m), Aasvoëlberg (354 m) and Spioenkop (340 m) would become islands.

Areas around Knysna estuary would be flooded with a sea level rise of 1 metre.

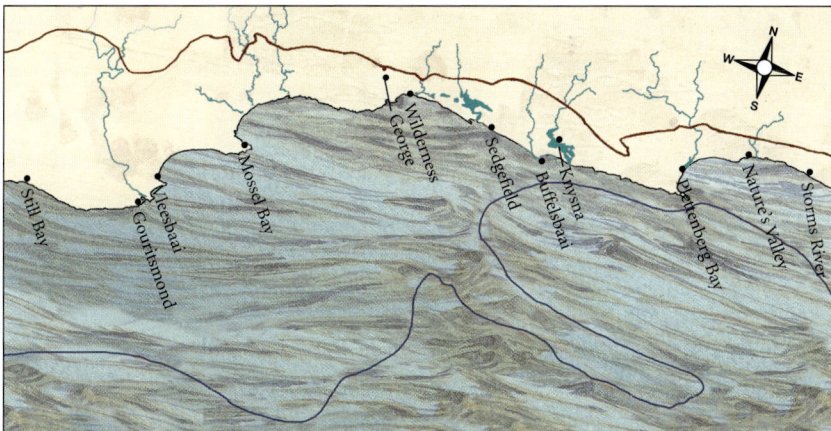

Sea Levels

— Ancient high sea level, often along the mountains

— Present coastline

— Low cretaceous coastline

7

WONDERS OF THE SEA

The coastline and its inhabitants are affected by the ocean's currents, waves, winds and climate. The processes that shaped the coast as we see it today, took millions of years, and still continue to alter it. The daily, weekly, and monthly levels of the sea change with tides.

These are the result of the combined gravitational pull of the Sun and the Moon acting on the water of the Earth's oceans. The tide inside an estuary is always later than the tide in the open sea, in the same area. This is because the restriction of the inlet slows down the changes in water level.

Early inhabitants of the Garden Route (page 106) utilised the tides by building fish traps, which local people still use today. As the tide recedes fish are trapped within the man-made walls, and the people simply collect their meal of fish.

Tides

There are basically two types of tides which alternate through the month – Spring and Neap tides.

Spring tides

Spring tides occur at full and new moon, at which times the Sun, Moon and Earth lie in a straight line. The water that lies along this line is pulled up higher because of the combined gravitational forces. The levels of water of oceans not on this line, are therefore correspondingly lower. Thus at any one time, the tide is particularly high at one place, and particularly low at another.

Neap tides

Neap tides occur when the Sun, Earth and Moon form a 90° angle. This happens when the Moon is in the first and last quarters. At this time the pull on the water in the oceans is more evenly distributed around the Earth. Thus there is less difference between high and low tide levels, all around the world.

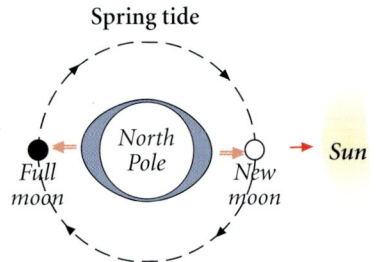

Spring tide

Full moon — North Pole — New moon — Sun

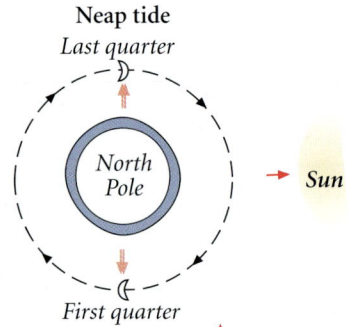

Neap tide
Last quarter
North Pole — Sun
First quarter

↑ Gravitational pull Sun
↑ Gravitational pull Moon

Rocks near Mossel Bay exposed at low spring tide

Mussel beds (page 54) are exposed at low tide. Collectors' note: each person is allowed a limited quota.

8

The relationship between ocean and estuarine tides is seen particularly well in the Keurbooms and Knysna estuaries. The Garden Route's tidal range is called micro-tidal, because there is generally less than 2 metre difference in the water-line between spring high and spring low tides. This controls the type of estuaries and beaches that can form.

False Plum Anenomes (page 51) have adapted to survive in the ever-changing intertidal zone.

In the Southern Hemisphere, as seen from Earth, a *C* moon ☾ is a **C**limbing, waxing moon, and a *D* moon ☽ is a **D**eclining, waning moon.

People are often fascinated to see that wherever they are the light of the Moon travels directly towards them over water.

Freak Waves

Freak waves can occur anywhere, at any tide, at any time of the year, and have a devastating effect on anything in their path. At any one time and place there may be a number of simultaneous, but different, swell-patterns. Sometimes two or more swell-crests happen to coincide. The resultant wave's height will be the sum of the coinciding, individual wave heights.

In the Garden Route, where there are usually moderate 2 metre swells, there could suddenly be a 4 metre or even 6 metre wave. These short-lived, unusually high swells can become 'freak waves'. Be aware! A freak wave can occur at any place where there is deep water near to the shoreline, e.g. at the foot of a sea-cliff, or on the rocks at the sea's edge. There are a number of places along the Garden Route where freak waves have claimed lives or caused serious injury. They occur at Mossel Bay, Herolds Bay, Victoria Bay, the Knysna Heads, Robberg and along the Otter Trail on the Tsitsikamma coast. When a freak wave breaks, it can flood the adjacent shoreline or rocks and wash away the unwary. There is no warning. The wave rises out of the sea, surges forwards, breaks and is gone.

Plum Anenome (page 51) is also an intertidal creature.

WONDERS OF THE SEA

THE POWER OF WAVES

Most people presume that a swell is a moving wall of water. This is not true. An ocean swell is the transport of energy: movement of actual water, sand and pebbles only occurs near the shore itself. A storm transfers energy from the blowing wind to the water, creating swells. These move along the surface of the ocean for hundreds to thousands of kilometres. In shallow water the swell rapidly changes to a wave, and moves stones and sand along the beach. Thus initial storm energy is transferred into erosion that carves a shoreline.

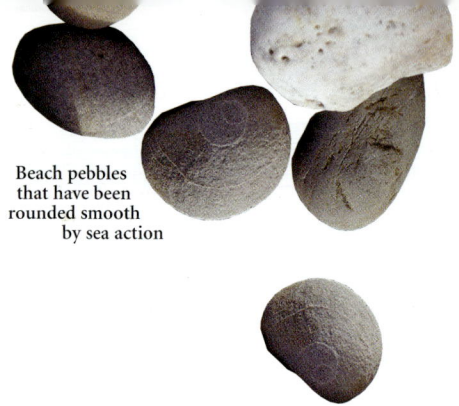

Beach pebbles that have been rounded smooth by sea action

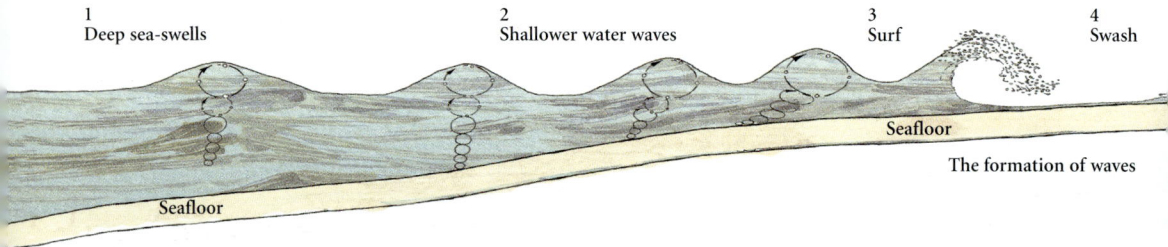

1
Deep sea-swells

2
Shallower water waves

3
Surf

4
Swash

Seafloor

The formation of waves

Seafloor

1. Deep Sea

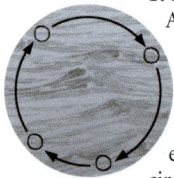

Water particles moving in a circle due to swell energy

A swell moves energy in the open ocean. The mass of water through which it travels remains in virtually the same place. Swells only appear to be moving – what we see is energy moving through the water. The passage of this energy causes the water particles to move in circles. They travel up the approaching swell's slope, slightly along the crest, down the swell's receding slope and back to the starting point, in the trough. Below the surface, this circular movement rapidly reduces to nothing. As a result the effect of the swell here is only felt on, and near, the surface. The deep seafloor is not affected by passing swells.

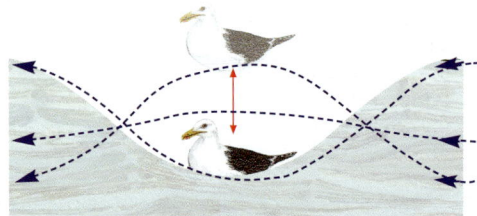

A floating bird or boat will show how little the water moves. In deep water they remain bobbing up the crests and down the troughs of swells. A human swimming, or on a surf-board, will do the same.

The slow-moving Southern Right Whale out in the deep sea

10

2. Shallow Water

When an ocean swell enters shallow coastal waters, it loses some of its energy by dragging against the seafloor. This slows the lower portion. The upper portion, however, continues to move.

This pushes a wave-crest upwards, steadily higher, as it rushes into shallower and shallower water. The wave increasingly transfers energy to the seafloor, and sand and pebbles are moved.

Swells entering shallow water at Plettenberg Bay form regular waves in the surf-zone.

3. Surf-zone

When the water is only a few metres deep, the wave-crest over-balances, crashes down, and a wall of turbulent, moving water surges towards the beach. Here the final swell-energy is used up, and a great deal of erosion and movement of sand and stones takes place. Eventually the thousands of waves that break on the shore every day, carrying abrasive particles in the water, erode the shore to a smooth, wave-cut platform, or to a sea-cliff, or to a bay.

4. Swash-zone

The swash rushing up and down a sandy beach sorts the sand grains to a uniform size, and smooths the beach to a flat, even surface.

Surf smashing on the rocks near Storms River

The wave's last energy is used up as swash.

WONDERS OF THE SEA
CURRENTS AND WAVES

The Garden Route is a transitional area. It is influenced by both the cold Benguela and the warm Agulhas currents. Most of South Africa has summer rainfall, and the south-western Cape has winter rain. The Garden Route has both.

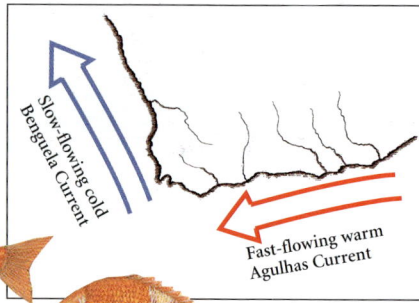

Slow-flowing cold Benguela Current

Fast-flowing warm Agulhas Current

Currents that occur along the southern Africa coastline. The Garden Route is affected by both.

Benguela Current
The Benguela Current flows north from the Antarctic up the west coast of South Africa. The water is cold and therefore the air is dry. Rain is unusual in the south-west Cape in the summer, and occurs with the onset of cold, wet conditions, associated with the powerful cold fronts of winter.

Red Roman (page 47) are endemic to the warmer Agulhas current coastline.

Agulhas Current
The Agulhas Current flows south from the equator, bringing warmth, moisture and summer rain from the tropics. By the time the Agulhas reaches the Garden Route, it is flowing east to west. Summer rainfall decreases because the current loses heat as it moves west.

Doublesash Butterflyfish (page 47) occur in the southern African waters affected by both the Benguela and Agulhas currents.

Garden Route Climate
The Garden Route is also a transitional rainfall area. It is here that the winter rainfall pattern, (from Mossel Bay westwards), changes to summer rainfall experienced in Port Elizabeth northwards. The area can experience strong south-westerly winds throughout the year. These are the main dune-forming winds of the region (see pages 20 - 23). During summer, easterly and south-easterly winds can raise high waves in the east-facing bays. This results in significant erosion of sandy beaches (see pages 18 - 19).

During stormy weather the Mossel Bay Lighthouse warns ships of the rocky coastline.

The pattern of swell-sets that arrives at the coastline can be most complex, and a simple pattern is rare.

Wave Patterns

Furry-ridged Triton (page 57)

Storms in the Antarctic Ocean produce enormous sets of swells. They sweep across the open ocean from the south-west, travelling for thousands of kilometres. In their death-throes they finally disperse their energy as surf, pounding the Garden Route coastline. This has been the pattern ever since the Indian Ocean was first fully developed (page 6). Near the coast, local, easterly storms can create quite large, but short-lived, swell-sets.

The size of swells depends on how hard the wind blew, for how long, over what surface area of water, and over what depth. This south-westerly pattern has helped to form many distinctive features of this coastline. In particular read about wave-cut platforms and fossil cliffs (page 14), half-heart bays (page 16 - 17) and dunes (pages 20 - 23).

Swells breaking onto a flat sandy beach

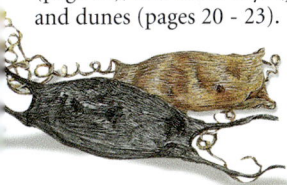

The energies of the currents and waves wash up many shells and other interesting treasures along the high water mark (pages 54, 55). For example the Mermaid's Purse (left) and the Pink-rayed Limpet (right).

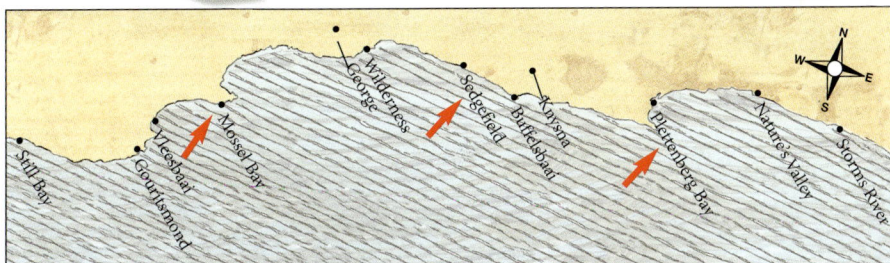

Swell Direction
The prevailing wind is from the south-west. In addition the most common swell-pattern from the Antarctic is also from the same direction.

13

WONDERS OF THE COASTLINE

The Garden Route is one of South Africa's most beautiful recreational areas – and it is only due to a unique coastal platform that this is so.

From Mossel Bay to Storms River, this idyllic platform lies between high mountains to the north, and the sea to the south, offering a vast array of opportunities for leisure and entertainment. Understanding how it was formed is fascinating.

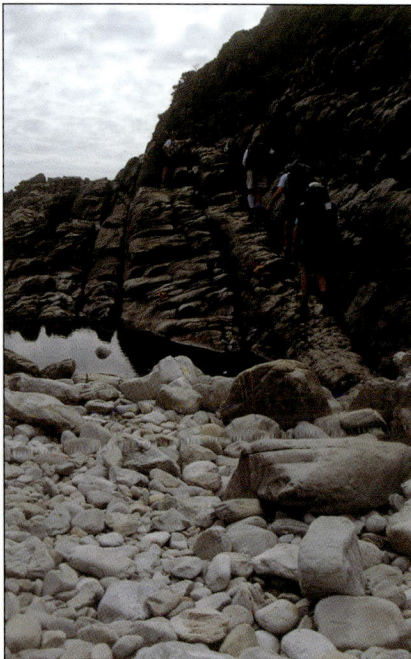

Hikers negotiating the sheer rock face, eroded by the power of water.

The Wave-cut Platform and Cliffs

As the sea level rises, it moves the abrasive surf-zone 'inland', and when it falls, the surf-zone moves further away. This see-saw changes the coastline continually (page 7).

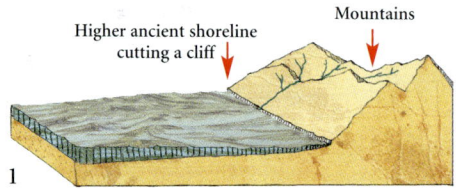

1. Over many millions of years sea level was repeatedly as much as 300 metres higher than now. For a long time the shoreline was at the foot of the Outeniqua and Tsitsikamma mountains.

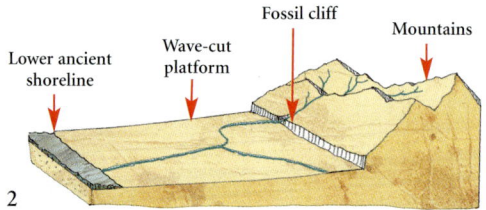

2. Later, over millions of years, the sea repeatedly fell and rose again. Each time it fell it revealed a wave-cut seafloor, bounded by steep cliffs where the shoreline had been. Cliffs form along the shoreline when the vertical jointed, hard, Table Mountain quartzite (TMQ) blocks are undercut by the surf. The eroded blocks fall into the sea, leaving a very steep cliff face.

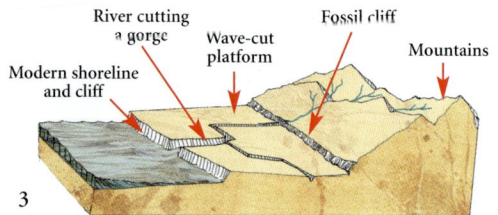

3. At the present position of sea level, we can enjoy the benefits of living on a remarkably flat, coastal platform. The slope of the platform is on average 1:300 seaward, and it varies in width from about 2 km to 30 km.

(M)

Southern Rock Agama (page 86)

Wave-cut platform

14

Sandy Beaches

Where the seafloor has a gentle, even, offshore slope, the waves tend to form a wide surf-zone. The waves start to break some distance away and each surf-wall keeps on rolling in, shedding energy all the way to the beach itself. This is a common scene on sandy beaches such as Hartenbos, Glentana, Sedgefield, Goukamma and Plettenberg Bay. Sandy beaches may develop offshore sand-bars during seasonal changes. This occurs when beach sand is moved offshore rather than along the shore. An offshore sand-bar can be recognised by a double surf-zone. The first surf-zone forms where the larger waves break over the sand-bar. This surf then reforms into swells that eventually break again as a second surf-zone closer to the beach itself. Offshore sand-bars commonly develop off the sandy beaches listed above.

The sandy beach at Great Brak River is a source of sand for the dunes.

African Black Oystercatchers (page 90) nest on sandy or rocky beaches.

Rocky Beaches

Where the seafloor slopes steeply, the swells come close inshore, then break suddenly. In extreme cases, for example at a sea-cliff, the breaking water is bounced off the cliff-face and actually pushes off to sea, causing great interference with the incoming swells. This can be seen off the Tsitsikamma coast. These beaches can be dangerous because of the up-rushing surf and the powerful return flow.

Modern Cliffs

The abrasive surf is a most efficient tool for etching the shoreline shape, depending on the nature of the rock. The straight shoreline of the Tsitsikamma coastline, and the steeply vertical cliffs, are a direct consequence of the very hard, layered and faulted nature of the Table Mountain quartzite (TMQ) in the area.

Abrasive surf at Storms River

Modern sea-cliffs to the west of Marine Drive overlooking the Otter Trail

15

WONDERS OF THE COASTLINE

CREATIVE WATER EROSION

Water itself has no cutting power. As it moves, however, it picks up particles of sand, or pieces of rock, and these have the power to abrade surfaces. Particles in suspension in the waves act on the coastline and create wave-cut platforms, or cliffs. This is similar to imagining that sandpaper only has an effect because of the sand!

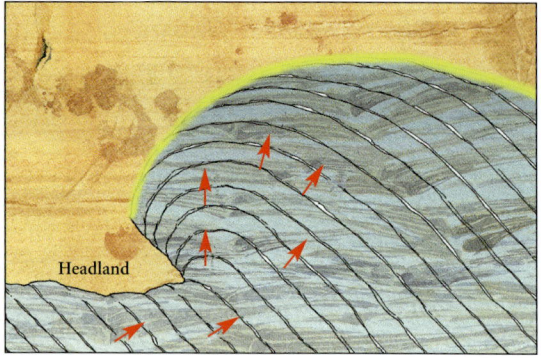

Refraction

← Direction of swells refracting around the headland

— Sandy beach in half-heart bay

Pink-lipped
Topshell
(page 54)

Variegated
Topshell
(page 54)

Refraction

It is easier to understand refraction once you have read how swell-energy is lost in shallow water, as the swell drags on the seafloor (see pages 10 - 11). When a swell-system approaches the coast at an angle, that part of the swell that meets the shallower coast first, slows down. This slower moving section does not travel forwards with the rest of the swell, but deflects, or 'refracts', until it eventually becomes a wave parallel with the shore. At a headland the swell breaks as a wave, and curls around the obstruction. The remainder of the swell continues forward, in its original direction, at the same speed. All along the curve of a bay, the end of the swell travelling in the shallow water refracts on the seafloor and curls around until the waves approach the shore parallel to a beach.

Wave refraction at the sea entrance to Knysna Estuary

Looking south-west over Buffelsbaai – a classic half-heart bay

Venus Ear
(page 56)

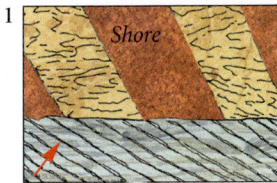

Half-heart (Log-spiral) Bays

1. The ancient Garden Route coastline consisted of alternating areas of harder TMQ and softer Cretaceous mudstone and sandstone (see pages 6 - 7). As the newly formed Indian Ocean changed to its present shape, the sea swells increasingly approached from the south-west.

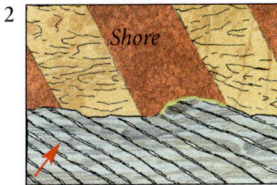

2. Over millennia, countless waves beat against the shore, eroding it slowly but surely. The resistant TMQ remained as headlands, and the Cretaceous mudstone and sandstone formed bays.

3. As the waves refracted around the headlands, the bays were deeply eroded into the distinctive half-heart shape we see today. The bays are sculpted on the northern side of the headlands.

Sea	Cretaceous mudstone & sandstone
Table Mountain quartzite	Swell direction
	Half-heart bays

The half-heart shape of bays formed by refracted swells are a precise mathematical curve called a logarithmic spiral – thus a 'log-spiral' bay. This is a similar mathematical spiral that is seen in whirlwinds, whirlpools, pinecones, spiral galaxies, and in sea shells (see examples on these pages, and Ram's Horn Shell on right).

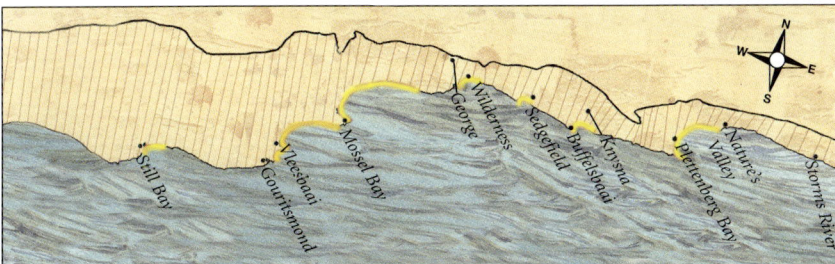

Coastline Features

- Half-heart bays
- Fossil cliffs
- Wave-cut platform

WONDERS OF THE COASTLINE

BEACHES AND CURRENTS

Coastal features are created through the interaction of waves, local coast-hugging currents and tides. Beaches offer superb opportunities for recreation, and understanding the processes can certainly increase your fun and your safety too. Refer to grid page 136 for information on the different beaches.

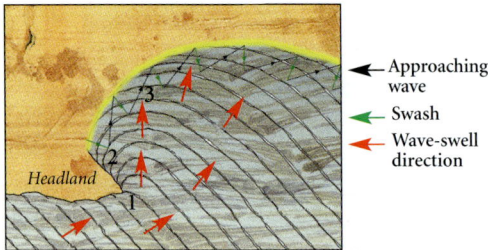

Along the beach the movement of sand continues in a zigzag pattern between each up and down swash. The longshore current nudges the sand grains, or other floating matter, in one direction, down-current, all the time.

Horn-eyed Ghost Crabs (page 54) can be seen moving sidewards along the shoreline.

Longshore Drift

Close inshore, in the surf-zone, the longshore current moves sand from beach to beach, continuously, like a natural conveyor belt. The longshore current is particularly effective where wave refraction is well developed, like around headlands. The turbulence of the breaking surf here helps to keep sand grains in suspension so that the longshore current can move them (see Refraction, page 16).

1. The concentrated surf at a headland lifts sand into suspension and provides energy for transport.

2. This energy from the refraction at the headland drives the current strongly into the bay.

3. The current weakens in the bay, and its load of sand is dropped to form a sandy beach.

A longshore drift may be responsible for the erosion of large quantities of beach sand. Along the Garden Route it can move more than a hundred thousand cubic metres of sand past a given point per year. That represents a pile of sand 50 m long, 50 m wide and some 40 m high! Swimmers are often well aware of the longshore drift. On these occasions when they find themselves drifting down the shoreline, away from the point where they entered the water, they can assume the swell-energy at the nearby headland is particularly strong.

A longshore drift moves sand along bays like at Gerickes Point, Sedgefield.

Sandy tombolo linking Robberg and The Island on the right

Tombolos

Where a sandy beach connects an island to the mainland, a tombolo is created. Its distinctive hourglass outline is the result of waves refracting around both sides of an island onto the tombolo beach. There are very few tombolos in South Africa. Possibly the best example is the beach at The Island on the south side of Robberg. Here refraction causes the surf to curl around both sides of The Island. At the tombolo beach, waves actually approach each other from opposite sides. The resulting double curvature of the tombolo shows a half-heart and its mirror image, which is very rare. These beaches are the mathematical curves of two sets of refracted waves.

A Brown Mussel shell
(pages 51, 54),
filled with sand

Swell direction

Rip current

Rip Currents

From time to time, sandbars and gulleys form on the seafloor where there are breakers. The breaking waves can drive excess water close to the beach, and here, momentarily, the water is trapped.

The piled-up water quickly rushes back out to sea along a gulley, much faster that the normal backwash that tugs at a wader's legs. The stream lasts only a very short while and dissipates just seaward of the surf-zone. This is a rip current, and is responsible for many drownings when unwary swimmers get swept out to sea and panic. The secret is to relax, to wait for the rip current to stop, and then to float back with the incoming waves. Rip currents also develop in rocky areas. Where there is a gulley between two rocks that are low enough for a wave to break over them, and a small bay on the shore side, water can again be trapped. The pull of the receding surf causes a similar, dangerous rip current.

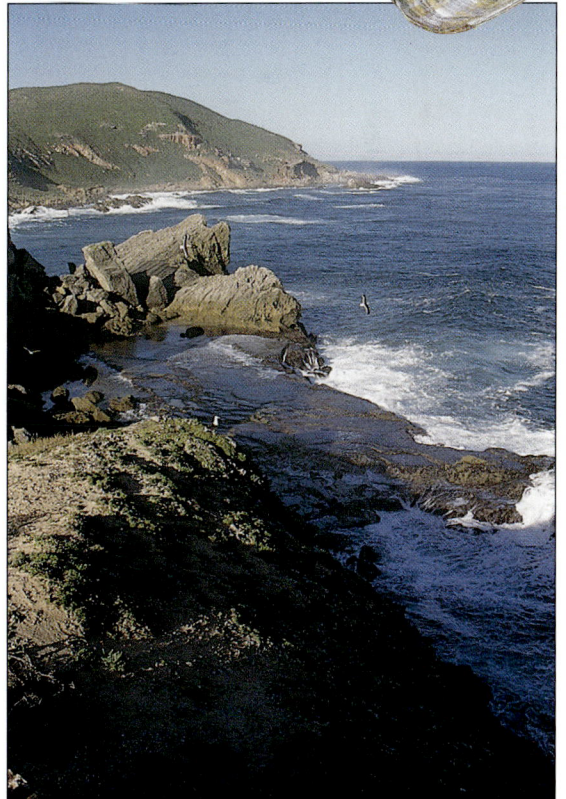

A typical rocky shore where
rip currents occur

19

ALL ABOUT DUNES

The dunes and lakes (pages 24 - 25) that form the landscape of the Wilderness are inextricably linked in their origin. The dunes are the fascinating result of sea level changes (see pages 6 - 9), whereas the lakes formed in the inter-dune valleys as the sea retreated.

Ancient dune-fields were formed repeatedly along this coast in the past. Some large ones were fossilised and are still visible today. Active dunes also occur, but they are generally small.

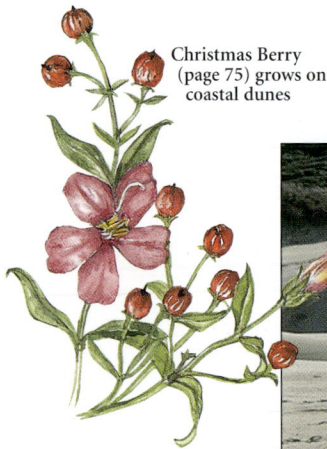

Christmas Berry
(page 75) grows on
coastal dunes

Dunes and Dune-fields

Wind action forms dunes which may range in size from less than a metre to two hundred metres high. Several kinds of dunes can form depending on wind speed, consistency of the wind, grain size, climate, presence of plants, and other conditions. Dunes and dune-fields commonly form along the coast where onshore winds blow across a sandy beach, sweeping sand inland. To move sand away, wind has to blow at a speed of at least 5 metres per second, which is 18 km/h (9,7 knots).

Cape Dune Molerat
(page 78)

The systematic downwind transport of sand, shown below, has the effect of moving the entire dune downwind. In the Garden Route area, small, coastal dunes usually move downwind at a rate of about 4 to 10 metres per year.

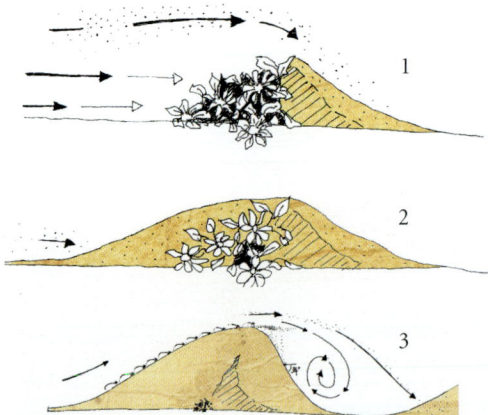

New and developing dunes

1. Any obstruction, like a plant, stone, rock, log, or even a house, which causes the wind to slow down, will cause air-borne sand to be deposited. This could be the start of a dune which, as it grows, will generate its own further growth, by slowing the wind.

2. As the dune grows, the sand is swept up the slightly convex, windward face.

3. The grains are blown beyond the crest, and once there, are drawn into the turbulence which forms in the lee of the dune. Here the speed drops, the wind can no longer keep the sand in suspension, and it is deposited on the lee slope (called the slipface).

Dunes forming around various plant species

Sea Pumpkin (page 74)

Wind Action lifting Sand – Saltation

Wind-blown sand is transported in a cloud of bounding, jumping grains close to the surface. Grains are in turn lifted, carried a distance, which is dependent on the wind speed, then dropped. As they hit the surface, they knock a number of other grains into the air. This spray of airborne grains is carried further along by the wind.

Anyone who has been on a sandy beach during a gale has felt the sting of the sand grains on their legs. This specific wind-sand action is called saltation.

Wind action lifting sand

Dunes forming the back-drop to Robberg Beach, Plettenberg Bay

ALL ABOUT DUNES

ACTIVE AND FOSSIL DUNES

The dunes and lakes are among the youngest of the landscape features along the Garden Route, being no more than 2 million years old. Dunes occur at those areas where sufficiently strong local winds can blow beach sand inland.

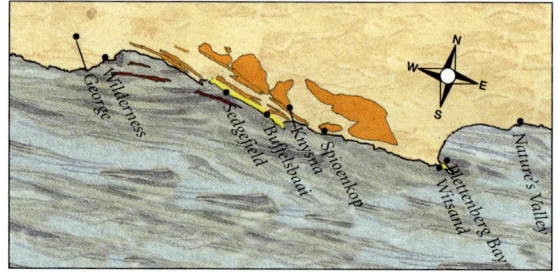

- ▮ Active dunes
- ▮ Fossil land dunes
- ▮ Fossil drowned dunes

Pig's Ear
(page 74)

Sea Lavender
(page 74)

Active Dunes – Climbing-falling Dune of Robberg

On the northern side of Robberg, is Witsand, an unusual dune, which is a clear white landmark. All year round the south-westerlies blow the sand up the southern slopes of Robberg from the tombolo beach at The Island. At the top the sand drops down the precipitous cliff onto a narrow beach or straight into the surf, 50 metres below. The powerful wind lifts many, many tons of sand every year up the full height of Robberg.

Witsand – the "falling" dune of Robberg

At Witsand itself, the dune slipface shows quite dramatically the characteristic 34° slope of all dunes. Here the sand that accumulates in the wind-shadow behind the crest, slides down the steep surface, under the influence of gravity. This area is unstable and can slump at any time. Do not walk on the slipface.

Fossil Dunes

The orientation and size of fossil dunes of the Garden Route prove that for the past 15 million years south-westerlies have been the most common winds. Among the largest of the fossil dune-fields is the one at Wilderness, which was formed during the Pleistocene, some 2 million years ago. They are easily recognised as dunes by their shape, even though they are now fully covered in vegetation. Dune-sand along the coast commonly contains a lot of shell fragments amongst the quartz sand grains. Rain water seeping through the dune dissolves some of the shell pieces and, when a dune is left undisturbed for a long enough period, this cements the sand grains together. The resultant hard mound of rock that is created is a fossil dune, that can survive for millions of years in the same place. Robberg, and particularly The Island, are among the places where the grainy, abrasive, easily eroded rocks that make up a fossil dune, are easy to see.

Sour Fig
(page 74)

22

Fossil Drowned Dunes

When sea level was lower, dune-fields developed on the then exposed seafloor, well beyond our present coastline. Over millennia they fossilised, and were later flooded and submerged by the rising sea. These dune-fields still exist, 2 - 7 km offshore, and can be traced with echo-sounding equipment on boats.

The best known section is a reef about 3,5 km offshore, 12 km long and about 2 km wide, which lies between Sedgefield and Buffelsbaai. Its crest is about 10 metres below the surface, and is regularly visited by fishermen (see diagram and map).

The slipface where wind-blown sand is deposited

Fossil Land Dunes

Two fossil dune-ridges (cordons), can be recognised clearly as the lines of hills in the Wilderness lake-land. The fossil dunes between Groenvlei and the sea are about 200 metres high from base to top, which makes them the highest in South Africa. The road to Map of Africa, near Wilderness, winds its way up the sea-cliff, and here there are wonderful vantage points for viewing the lakes and dune-ridges. Dolphin Point, on the N2 between George and Wilderness, also offers a spectacular vista to the east.

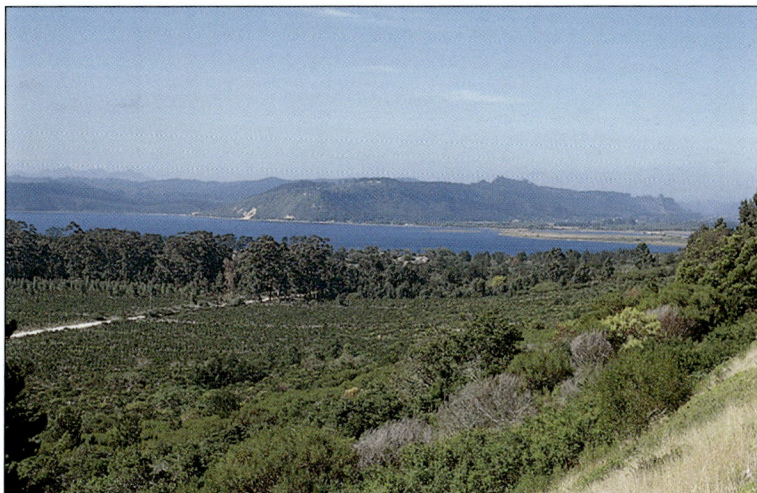

Looking towards Spioenkop over Swartvlei

Spioenkop

The most inland fossil dunes occur at Spioenkop, shown in the picture above, across Swartvlei Lake. The dunes reach an elevation of almost 350 metres, because they lie on the wave-cut platform, which locally itself has an elevation of about 200 metres above sea level (see diagram below).

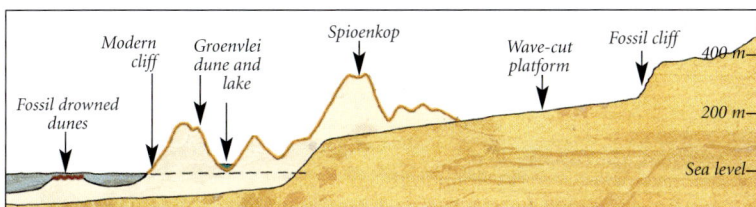

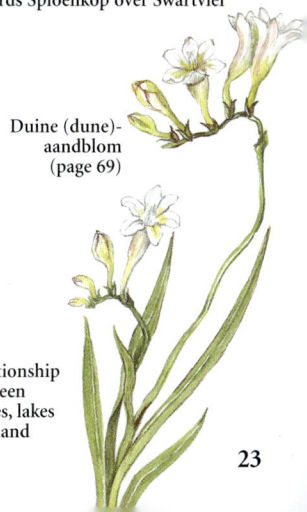

Duine (dune)-
aandblom
(page 69)

Relationship
between
dunes, lakes
and land

23

LAKES

The Wilderness lake-land is not only scenically beautiful, but also offers wonderful recreational opportunities. The lakes are too small and too shallow to develop any large waves, regardless of wind strength, and are therefore ideal for boating activities like canoeing, kayaking and wind-surfing.

Grey Herons
(page 94) are a
common sight around the
Lakes in the Garden Route area.

The Wilderness Lakes

These were formed by the natural damming of water in the valleys, between two dune-ridges.
The lakes are particularly interesting because each has a different working structure. The Knysna and Swartvlei lagoons are open to the sea, and are tidal. They therefore function more like estuaries than true lakes (see page 32). There is a small map on page 31 to show the Lake area.

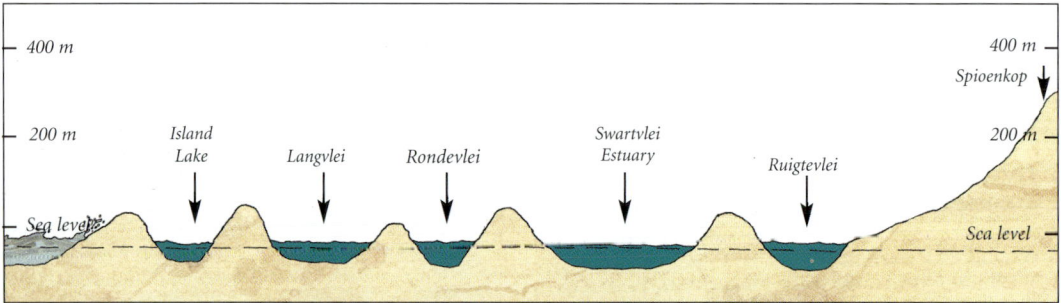

Some of the Garden Route Lakes showing their levels are, on average, consistant with sea level.

Looking east over the Wilderness lakes and dunes

Dune Slack Rush
(page 123),
a sedge that is
dominant along
the banks of
Swartvlei at
Sedgefield (hence
the name).

Swartvlei, a popular recreation area

Water Beetle,
Family Dytiscidae
(20 mm)
Water beetles occur in
freshwater rivers and
lakes, like Groenvlei.
They can fly and swim
underwater. They use
their oar-like back legs
to swim, and to trap fresh
air in the space between
the wings and abdomen.
This air acts as a
waterlung.

Island Lake, Langvlei and Rondevlei

Island Lake is connected to the Touw River Estuary by the Serpentine, a
meandering channel that regularly feeds tidal water into and out of its opening.
The Touw in flood can back up the Serpentine, raising Island Lake's water level
by more than 2 metres in 12 hours or less. A narrow channel connects Island
Lake, Langvlei and Rondevlei. Therefore the latter two are also salty. The filling
of these lakes is not only via the Touw estuarine water. It is also by underground
seepage, possibly even of sea water, through the barrier dunes.

Groenvlei

Groenvlei is by contrast a completely freshwater lake, which gives rise to the
conspicuous reed growth around its shores. Groenvlei's water is only obtained
through run-off and seepage from the surrounding dunes. In some maps of the
1940s, it is marked as 'seasonal', indicating its dependence on run-off from
nearby dunes when it rains.

Estuarine
Roundherring
(page 48)
have adapted
to freshwater
conditions
in Groenvlei,
which was once
connected to
the sea.

Looking across Groenvlei Lake, from the N2 to the Groenvlei
vegetated fossil dunes.

RIVER POWER

*Rivers, their valleys, gorges, estuaries
and river-mouths are dramatic
landforms along the Garden Route.
The flowing water of rivers
significantly influences the landscape.
They scour away rocks and soil, and
then deposit the sediments further
downstream. Rivers have
transformed the local landscape
many times before, and will do
so again.*

River pebbles, pounded to shape
by the power of river water

The Power of Rivers

The primary driving force of rivers is, of course,
gravity. Rivers do most of their erosive work in their
beds. Normally they are not efficient during times
when flow is low, or as they get close to sea level.
While in flood, however, they grind the bedrock away,
and transport their sediment to the sea.

There is indirect erosion on the valley slopes by rain
and gravity. Rocks and soil wash and slide into the
flowing water below, and widen the valley sides.

Rivers world-wide work towards establishing their
own stable river gradient. This has a steeper initial
section, flattening out towards the coasts. The slope
is dependent on the height the river drops, and the
distance to the coast.

The Twee-riviertjies waterfall, near Storms River, demonstrates the power of water

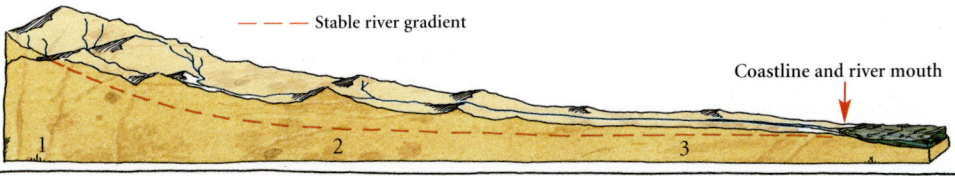

Stable river gradient

Coastline and river mouth

1. Along the Garden Route, the upper sections of rivers commonly have narrow valleys and a steep gradient. Here the water flows fast, like in mountain torrents. Rapids and waterfalls are common.

2. Downstream the valleys are commonly wider, and the river-flow becomes more sedate. Erosion is therefore more lateral, and the sides of the valleys tend to be much wider.

3. At the end of its journey, near the sea, river-flow is slow. Rivers that enter the sea through Table Mountain quartzite (TMQ) tend to form gorges, while those which finish on softer rock tend to form estuaries. At the estuary the direction of river-flow can be reversed temporarily, while the tide comes in.

Rejuvenation

While a river flows over land which is neither rising nor falling, relative to sea level, it will work to establish a stable river gradient. If, however, the sea level drops, the river 'rejuvenates'. This means that the river regains some of its 'youthful' energy. Its original mouth is now again **above** sea level and therefore needs to reconnect with the sea. It begins working at establishing a second stable river gradient, between its previous mouth, and the new sea level. All the larger rivers, e.g. Storms River, have already cut deep gorges in the elevated marine platform in their efforts to re-establish their mouths at the new sea level.

Many small rivers along the Tsitsikamma flow entirely on the wave-cut platform. Because they have a small catchment area, and the platform has a low gradient, their present erosive power is limited. They have not yet cut gorges, nor do they have estuaries. All of them, however, have the advantage of entering the sea at the modern sea-cliff, and this will help increase their slope by rejuvenation. It won't be long before they cut their own mini-gorges.

At least one of these little rivers, the Twee-riviertjies, about three hours walk along the beginning of the Otter Trail, is visibly demonstrating its potential vigour, tumbling into the sea by a waterfall (see left). The picture on the right shows a young river, rising on the platform, with enough energy to ultimately cut a mini-gorge (see pages 30 - 31).

Brakenhill Falls on the Witels River near Knysna

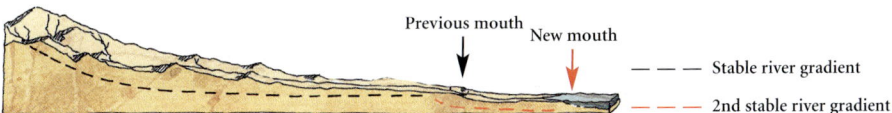

Previous mouth   New mouth

Stable river gradient

2nd stable river gradient

RIVER POWER

RIVER PATTERNS

Even the larger rivers along this coast, except the Gourits, rise either in the Tsitsikamma, Outeniqua or Langkloof mountain ranges, or on the wave-cut platform between the ranges and the sea. This means their catchment areas are relatively small. Only the Gourits has the capacity to regularly discharge a large amount of water into the sea. Being very local rivers, that do not pass through heavily industrialised and urban areas, most of the water is unusually clean and unpolluted.

The 'pattern' of the rivers and their tributaries changes according to whether they flow across Table Mountain quartzite (TMQ), granite or Cretaceous mudstone. (see map).

Eastern Cape Redfin Minnow (page 126) is threatened. It is endemic, and found in the coastal rivers of this area.

The tree-like (dendritic) pattern is typical of rivers that drain Cretaceous mudstone and sandstone areas, as well as the granite area near George.

The Gourits River

This is the largest and longest river in the Garden Route, draining from the Oudtshoorn area beyond the watershed of any of the other rivers here. The Gourits River cuts a gorge through the raised floor of a fossil half-heart bay that originally lay west of Mossel Bay, (see page 17). The original TMQ headland that protected this half-heart bay is at the Aasvoëlberg, and the Gourits has cut a gorge even through this obstruction in its way.

The Rivers of the George Plain

All the rivers of the George plain, including the Little Brak River to the west, are young rivers developed entirely on the wave-cut platform. The George plain lies on granite. This gives rise to the distinctive tree-like drainage pattern seen in most of the rivers drawn on the map above.

Kaffirkuils River at Still Bay

The Piesang River

This small, young river has its own somewhat lopsided gorge. The river flows through a Cretaceous mudstone basin. It has resistant TMQ on the north side of the 'gorge', whereas, the other side of the valley has a gentle slope. This side is mudstone and sand-stone, which is unable to maintain the steep slopes characteristic of the TMQ.

The Goutrits River near its estuary

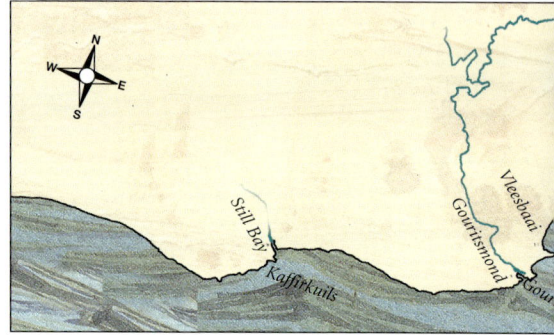

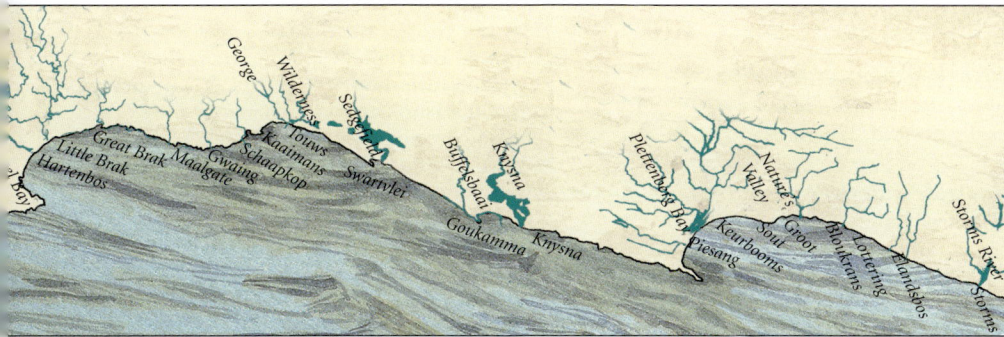

The Keurbooms River

The headwaters of the Keurbooms River come from the Langkloof, north of the main Tsitsikamma mountain range. This river was already flowing when sea level was 300 metres above its present level. The placid waters of its estuary hide the tortuous journey of the mother stream through the inland mountain valleys. Its gorge is spectacular and well worth a voyage upstream to enjoy the unspoilt, unpolluted beauty.

Keurbooms River, near Aventura Eco Plettenberg, peacefully reflects its surroundings

The Storms River System

The Storms River has a steep, mountain stream gradient over most of its course, that has helped it cut its magnificent gorge. In addition it happened to strike a convenient weak zone to use as a bed. Its water flows vigorously and turbulently, especially during flood, when it does most of its erosive work. The near-vertical side walls of the Storms River gorge are a testimony to the hardness of the TMQ, as well as an indication of the power of the river. The other interesting thing to note is how the main tributary, the Witteklip River, meets the Storms River at nearly 90°, because of the pattern of weak zones in the TMQ.

Cape Clawless Otter (page 81) found in most pristine river areas

The upper reaches of Storms River

29

GORGES

All the gorges look more or less alike, and although their depth varies, it is generally around 230 metres.

The very narrow width of a gorge valley, compared with its depth, and the near-vertical layers of Table Mountain quartzite (TMQ) that form the side walls, are spectacular. The numerous cracks and joints in the rock, along which the river excavated its channel, are easy to see in many places.

Krantz (cliff) Aloe (page 73) grow on the steep slopes of rocky gorges.

How the Gorges were made

For a very long time, possibly for more than 50 million years, the local shoreline was at the foot of the Tsitsikamma Mountains. During this time, surf erosion formed a wide, submerged, wave-cut platform. From time to time sea level dropped for a while, exposing the platform to the erosive action of the rivers.

When sea level drops, the natural response of the rejuvenated river is to deepen its valley (see page 27). Valley deepening takes place at a much faster rate than widening of the valley sides. In the very hard Table Mountain quartzite (TMQ), the valley sides remain nearly vertical. The repeated process of sea level drop and rise helped the rivers to cut the gorges to their present depth. The process continues at present, and valley deepening is still more important than widening.

Cape-chestnut (page 60) grows in river valleys.

Active gorge-cutting at the magnificent viewsite, Map of Africa, near Wilderness

Gorges made History

Since the earliest humans enjoyed the benefits of the wave-cut platform and its bounty, the gorges have formed a major obstacle to human travel in the region.

Tree-fuchsia (page 64)

Hunter-gatherers, and later herders, followed animal paths to make their way down and up the precipitous cliff faces. The gorges formed natural barriers that both limited and protected early human endeavour along the coast. When European settlers arrived, the flat platform was ideal for farming. However, because travel along the coast was limited by the gorges, a harbour was developed at Knysna, despite its hazardous entrance at The Heads. Because of the insurmountable engineering problems, a railway connection was never established across the gorges, except over the Gourits.

Even the original mountain road passes were a major accomplishment. The road makers also tried to follow the original elephant paths through the valleys as closely as possible. The first gorge to be bridged was the Storms River (mid-1950s), with the others following during the late 1970s.

These single-span concrete arch bridges are among the highest in Africa. They have revolutionised road travel along the Garden Route, and afford a spectacular grandstand view of the gorges up and down river. But the old roads that wind their way down the narrow valleys, to the bottom, and up the other side, are equally impressive. Driving these roads will show you how steep and deep the gorges are. You will be aware of the obstacle that they have presented to man and animal alike, for the past hundreds of thousands of years.

Up the Storms River gorge from its mouth

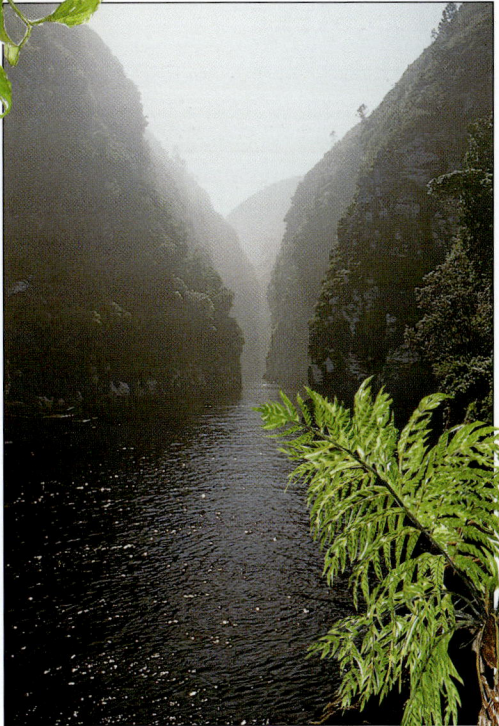

Forest Tree Fern (page 60)

The modern bridge over Groot River

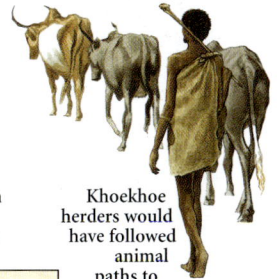

Khoekhoe herders would have followed animal paths to negotiate gorges.

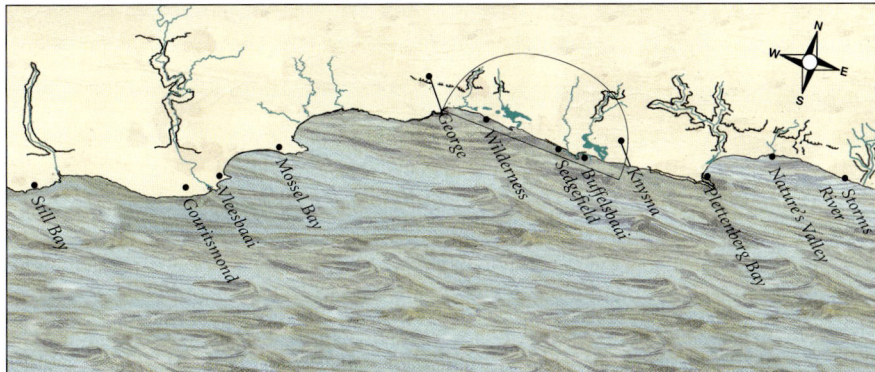

Lakes and Gorges

Gorges

Lake area

31

RIVERS MEET THE SEA

Near the places where rivers meet the sea we find river mouths and estuaries, and often wetlands. The differences are interesting.

Common Sand
Hermit Crab
(page 53)

Estuaries and Lagoons Estuaries develop where sea water and river water mix in the lower sections of the river during the change of the tides. Estuaries are very important breeding grounds for fish (pages 48 - 49).

The 'mouth' of an estuary is called the 'inlet', a name that stresses the significance of the influence of the in-flowing sea water during a rising tide. Along the Garden Route larger estuaries maintain open mouths. However, the small tidal range of the Garden Route coast causes many of the smaller estuaries to have a sand-bar across the inlet. These are not always open to the sea.

Knysna Seahorse
(page 48) is a
threatened species
that is found in the
Knysna estuary.

There are large estuaries with open inlets at Keurbooms-Bitou, Knysna, Swartvlei, Little Brak, Great Brak and Gourits.

Four estuaries that are closed at times are the Groot, Touw, Piesang and Hartenbos. Closed estuaries create more of a lagoon than a true estuary. When the end of a river has only a see page outlet to the sea, through sand blocking the mouth, it is called a lagoon.

Glasswort Samphire
(page 75)

The Knysna Estuary is unusual in that it has a fixed rocky inlet, The Heads.
In other ways, however, it functions much like estuaries with migrating inlets.

River Mouths

These develop where the river flows directly into the sea. The level of the river-bed is such that, even at high tide, hardly any sea water flows into the river-channel.

Many of the small rivers along the Tsitsikamma coast flow directly into the sea. The Kaaimans, one of the larger river-mouths, shows a dramatic plume of rusty brown forest water mixing with the white foam of the surf breaking in the mouth. This is particularly impressive during the ebb-tide, when the river-water streams conspicuously into the sea.

Common Whimbrel (page 95)

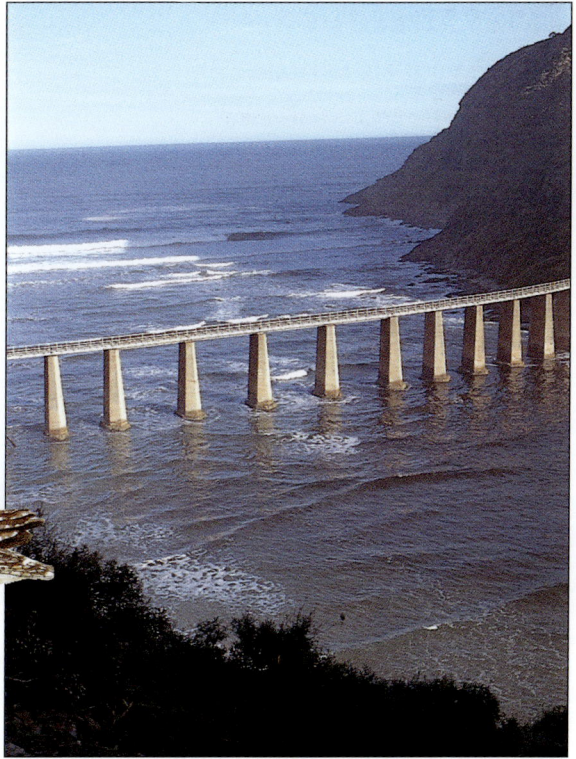

The Kaaimans River mouth at low tide

Wetlands

These are marshy areas, either fresh or brackish. They occur along the edges of estuaries and in more inland, low-lying areas, such as river flood-plains.

Wetlands are significant breeding grounds for various organisms, and form buffers for flood-waters. The flood-plain of the Bitou is an excellent example of a wetland. From the vantage point of a local hill slope, the snake-like meandering channels, and U-shaped oxbow lakes and marshes, testify to the changing conditions in the flood-plain.

The wetlands of the Touw and Serpentine rivers, at Wilderness, are equally interesting, with the same features.

Black-winged Stilts (page 95)

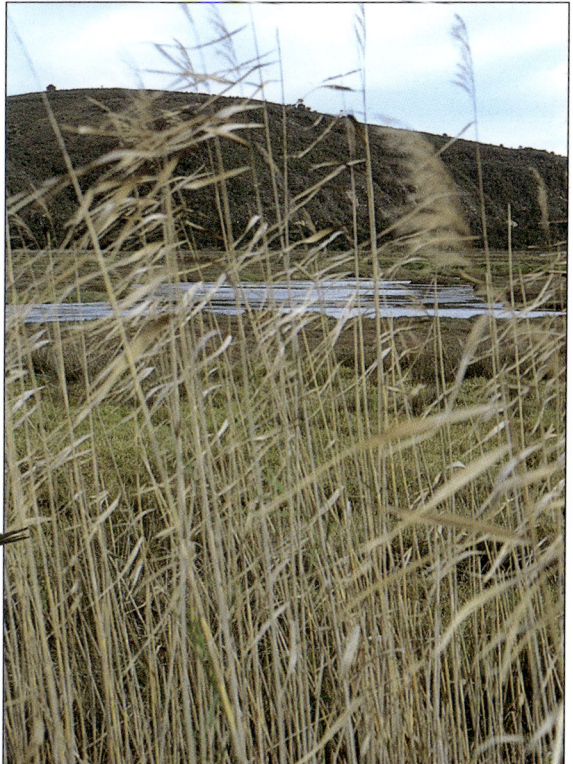

The excellent birding area of the Bitou wetlands

33

RIVERS MEET THE SEA

THE KEURBOOMS ESTUARY

Keurbooms is the most beautiful, and the best example of an estuary along this coast. It is easy to access, both along its land and sea shores. It is spectacular to look at, especially from the many vantage points along the Table Mountain quartzite (TMQ) hill on its south-western boundary. It is used here as an example of how estuaries work in general. Follow the numbers 1 - 7 to help you to understand the dynamic system of an estuary.

1. The Inlet

The appearance of the Keurbooms inlet changes often. Prior to 1915, it was at Lookout rocks, when a major river flood broke through at the northern end of the estuary. However, the new inlet immediately started migration southwards towards Lookout again, at a rate of a few metres per year. This is clearly seen in the erosion of the southern inlet bank, and the growth of the northern barrier beach (see 4).

It is likely that the process will repeat itself, should the Keurbooms come down again in a major flood.

Key to Keurbooms Estuary looking north

Giant Kingfisher (page 92) feed on Marsh and Mud Crabs (page 53).

2. The Flood-tidal Delta

At low tide prominent sandbanks are exposed opposite the inlet. Their shape changes all the time, but usually the delta is made up of one or more gracefully curved half-moons of sand. They are formed by seasand that is carried into the estuary by the rising tides – hence the name.

This is an unusual 'delta' because it lies on the landward side of the inlet. Conventional deltas develop on the seaward side. The constantly shifting sand makes it very difficult for burrowing animals to establish themselves and to live here.

Heart Urchins
(page 52)

3. Sub-tidal Channels

Even at low spring tide, the sub-tidal channels remain filled with water. The rush of water leaving the estuary causes turbulence in the inlet. The resultant erosion helps undercut the southern bank of the inlet, aiding its migration southwards.

4. The Barrier Beach

In its wake the migrating inlet leaves behind a barrier beach, which is a combination of beach and low dunes. The barrier beach is formed by waves and the longshore current (see pages 18 - 19). There is an established plant community on the southern part, but only a few pioneer plants live in the bare sand along the newly formed northern tip of the barrier.

Marsh Crab
(page 53)

There are other Barrier Beaches at some of the smaller estuaries, notably the Groot and the Touw. These barriers form faster than the rivers can breach them. The estuaries exchange sea water and fresh water by seepage, and are only infrequently, and for a short time, open to the sea.

5. Supra-tidal Flats

These flats are raised above normal high tide. A fascinating variety of salt-tolerant plants grow here. They are only covered by sea water during spring tide storms. A myriad of small burrowing crabs make their home here. This is also a superb birding area.

6. Inter-tidal Flats

These flats stretch for some distance upstream. Their surface is relatively flat and firm, and is characteristically rippled by the flowing water. They are home to shrimps and pencil-bait that make distinctive burrows in the sand.

7. Inter-tidal Lagoon

The south-western end of the estuary is a lagoon with no through-flow. The reed-banks along the shore indicate fresh water springs coming from the TMQ in the cliffs behind the lagoon. These are characterised by muddy sand, lots of estuarine Cape Eelgrass (*Zostera capensis*) and a large population of shells and other invertebrate animals. They burrow so extensively in the sand that anyone walking here sinks knee-deep into the maze of holes and burrows.

8. Direction to Lookout Rocks

9. Wave-cut Platform

See text on page 14 and map on page 19.

Sea Pumpkin (page 74)
is one of the pioneer
plants that stabilises sand.

SEA LIFE

There are so many miracles along the Garden Route coast it is no wonder that since the earliest days of hunter-gatherers in southern Africa this has been a mecca for human activity. Part of the appeal has always been the sea life that teams in the ocean itself, as well as along the shore.

The coastline consists of long stretches of sandy beaches interrupted by rocky shores and cliffs. Different zones occur along the beach – the richest zone with the most diversity is the intertidal zone (the area between low and high tide) which is exposed to continual wave action. Here animals thrive in abundance – snails and mussels lie hidden beneath the sand, while diverse invertebrate communities live on the rocks.

Out in the ocean there are a number of zones or habitats. The open water (pelagic region) supports animals like whales, game fish and jellyfish, while the ocean bottom (benthic region) is where creeping animals like Sand Prawns and Sea Urchins live. Rocky reefs can also form out in the deep ocean, on which many different organisms depend for survival.

> *Crustaceans and their shells, fish and mammals are all measured in length, unless otherwise stated.*

This Southern Right Whale could easily be mistaken for a barnacle-covered rock.

SEA MAMMALS

Although there is a great diversity of marine mammals occurring off the Garden Route coast (up to 40 species), the ones you are most likely to see are illustrated on these pages. Only one indigenous seal species occurs here, the rest are whales and dolphins. Like other mammals, these animals breathe air, are warm-blooded and give birth to live young, which they suckle. They have a thick layer of fatty blubber for insulation.

WHALES

Whale hunting has fortunately been banned since 1986, and there are also laws which prevent people from boating within 300 metres of whales. Some whales spend the summer near the Antarctic, feeding on krill (tiny shrimps) before migrating north to warmer waters for the winter.

For whale watching hotspots see page 136. Take a pair of binoculars and focus beyond and in the breakers to spot whales and dolphins.

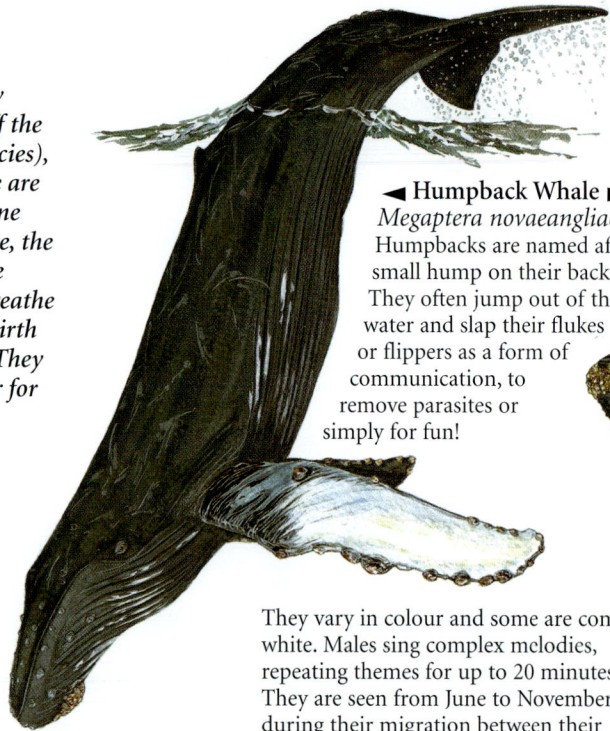

◄ **Humpback Whale** ►
Megaptera novaeangliae (15 m)
Humpbacks are named after the small hump on their backs. They often jump out of the water and slap their flukes or flippers as a form of communication, to remove parasites or simply for fun!

They vary in colour and some are completely white. Males sing complex melodies, repeating themes for up to 20 minutes. They are seen from June to November during their migration between their breeding grounds off Mozambique and their feeding grounds in the Antarctic.

Southern Right Whale ►
Eubalaena australis (14 - 16 m)
These are the most common whales off the southern coast. They were known as the 'right' whales to hunt because they are slow moving and float once killed, so it is easy to bring them back to shore. With hunting now banned, their population is slowly increasing. Barnacles and whale-lice attach themselves onto patches of raised rough skin on the whales' heads. Researchers use these pale-brown patches to identify individual whales. These whales are seen mostly during August and September, when the females calve in sheltered, sandy-bottomed bays. For three months, the calves drink 200 litres of milk a day to build up blubber for the long trip to the Antarctic. The illustration shows a female carrying her calf on her back.

Comparison of the whales depicted on this page

Southern Right Whale

The head has callosities (pale, rough patches of skin); each whale has a different pattern; long, narrow baleen plates.

The tail fluke is very broad – 3,5 m across; smooth trailing edges, curving inwards; pointed tips; distinct notch in centre; often seen.

The flippers are large, paddle-shaped and often seen.

No dorsal fin

Humpback Whale

The head has golf-ball sized knobs (with sensory hairs) on top of head and lower jaw; baleen is short and wide; head about 1/3 of body length; there are throat grooves.

The tail fluke has a broad, irregular, knobbly trailing edge; distinct notch; usually black on top and variable white patches underneath; each whale has a different pattern; often seen.

The flippers are very long, about 1/3 of body length; knobs on leading edge, notches on trailing edge; often seen; usually black on top and white underneath.

The dorsal fin is a low, stubby fin with hump in front, very variable; small humps behind fin towards tail.

Bryde's Whale

The head has three parallel ridges running from near tip of snout to near blow-hole; baleen is short and wide, and brownish or greyish; there are throat grooves.

The tail fluke is relatively broad; distinct notch in centre; slightly concave trailing edges.

The flippers are slender and short, about 1/10 of body length; pointed tips; not often seen.

The dorsal fin is prominent, erect and hooked; shark-like; variable; trailing edge sometimes frayed; situated about 2/3 of the way back along the body.

▼ Bryde's Whale
Balaenoptera edeni
(13 - 14 m)
Some of these whales are resident off the southern coast all year, while others migrate to equatorial waters. They are often seen 6 - 15 km offshore, in small groups of 5 - 6. They swim much faster than Southern Right Whales, often darting here and there to chase small fish such as anchovy, pilchard and squid. They also eat plankton.

SEA MAMMALS

WHALES AND DOLPHINS

Whales and dolphins are called Cetaceans, 37 species of which occur off southern Africa. Cetaceans surface to breathe air, blowing out a spout of air and water vapour as they do so. They can see both above and below the surface of the water by changing the lens shape in their eyes. There are two groups of Cetaceans, those with teeth, which mainly eat fish and squid, and those with comb-like baleen plates to strain plankton from the water. Both whales and dolphins jump out of the water (breach), and some whales slap the water with their tail flukes and flippers.

◄ Orca
Orcinus orca
(M 8,8 m; F 7,9 m)
Orca whales are often seen floating belly-up or jumping clear out of the water. They hunt in packs catching fish, squid, birds, seals and dolphins, and are sometimes called 'Killer Whales'. They will even attack large whales, but are not known to attack people. Like some other Cetaceans, they take care of injured companions.

Minke Whale ▲
Balaenoptera acutorostrata (9,2 - 9,8 m)
Minke Whales migrate to the Antarctic where they aggregate in large numbers during summer to feed on krill. Some females and calves may stay in warmer waters, where small fish become part of their diet. They are the smallest and most abundant of the baleen whales and are usually spotted when they leap clear out of the water, ending their breech in a huge splash. Promontories along the coast are usually the best places to spot this whale. Minke Whales may form a large part of the Killer Whale's diet in the Antarctic.

▼ False Killer Whale
Pseudorca crassidens (5,5 m)
Smaller and darker than true killer whales, these blunt-nosed whales may be seen jumping out of the water in a flat, low arc. They eat mainly fish and squid and live in small groups. They are attracted to boats, but do not usually follow them as they are slow swimmers.

◄ Cape Fur Seal
Arctocephalus pusillus pusillus
(M 2,2 m; F 1,6 m)
Fur Seals have thick coats of dark-brown to golden. These superb swimmers eat mainly fish, but also squid and mud prawns. Seals can also move on land and are quite skilled climbers. When hauling themselves out of the sea, they use the waves to help them up onto rocks.

Common Dolphin
Delphinus delphis (2,5 m)
These streamlined dolphins have a figure-of-eight pattern on each side, which is sometimes tinged with yellow. There is also a thin black line from the corner of the mouth to the flipper. They live in 'pods' of 20 to several hundred animals, following well-defined routes along the coast. They usually feed in deeper waters on fish, squid and cuttlefish, and can swim up to 20 knots, often following ships for long distances.

▼ Humpback Dolphin
Sousa plumbea (2,8 m)
Recognised by the hump below their back fin, they are hardy and less playful than other dolphins. They seldom jump, surf or follow ships. They form small groups, usually of 3 - 7, and catch fish around rocky reefs.

▼ Bottlenosed Dolphin ▲
Tursiops truncatus (2,6 - 3,3 m)
Bottlenosed Dolphins have a thin, pale line running from the eye to the flipper and short, stout snouts. They are usually seen off the coast surfing in the waves or feeding on fish and squid. They live in organised social groups of 10 - 60. They hunt together, herding the fish into a small area to catch them more easily.

Echolocation

Common Dolphin

Dolphins and other toothed whales navigate and find their food using echolocation. This means they produce high-frequency, pulsed sounds (clicks) which bounce back off solid objects, so they can find out where they are. They communicate with each other using a variety of other sounds – groans, moans and whistles. Baleen whales, such as the humpbacks, produce very low frequency sounds ('songs') that travel more than 10 km. These sounds are produced, not by a vocal cord, but via the respiratory system, especially the nasal cavity. The underwater sonar used by many ships and submarines can interfere with the echolocation and communication channels of Cetaceans, making it difficult for them to find their mates and locate feeding grounds.

Ecolocation - the above illustrates how, by use of high-frequency sounds, this Common Dolphin locates its food in the form of Zebra fish (page 46).

MAINLY MARINE FISH

The greatest mass of marine fish is found in the surface waters of the open sea. The greatest diversity is found in the coastal zone, where the fish display an amazing variety of form and colour. Marine fish are divided into two main groups, bony and cartilaginous fishes – the difference being in the structure of the skeleton.

CARTILAGINOUS FISH

Cartilaginous fish include the sharks, rays, sandsharks and sawfishes. Their skeletons consist of cartilage, which is what separates them from the bony fish (pages 44 - 47). They are all carnivorous with exceptionally good senses of hearing and smell (some sharks can hear up to a kilometre away). They also have a remarkable electrical detection system, which is very sensitive to vibrations and assists hunting.

People have used the oceans' renewable fish resources from the earliest times. The pressure on marine resources has increased so greatly in recent times that many fish species have suffered from over-fishing. The marine ecosystem is fragile, and its use as a sustainable resource must be based on an understanding of the biological processes that govern life in the oceans.

Comparison of sizes

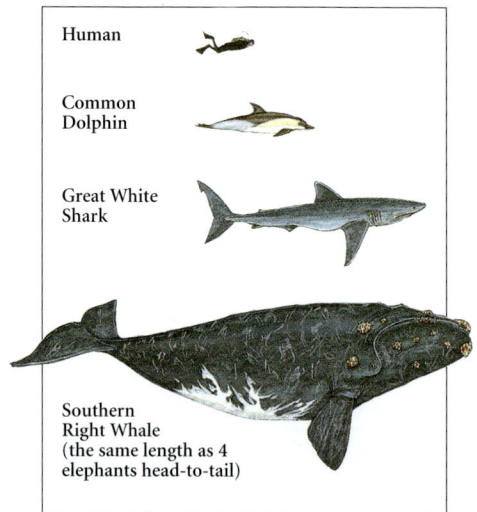

Human

Common Dolphin

Great White Shark

Southern Right Whale (the same length as 4 elephants head-to-tail)

▲ **Pyjama Shark (Striped Catshark)**
Poroderma africanum
(95 cm)
These sharks occur only in South Africa. They are usually found in rocky areas with shallow water where they feed at night on small reef fish and octopus.

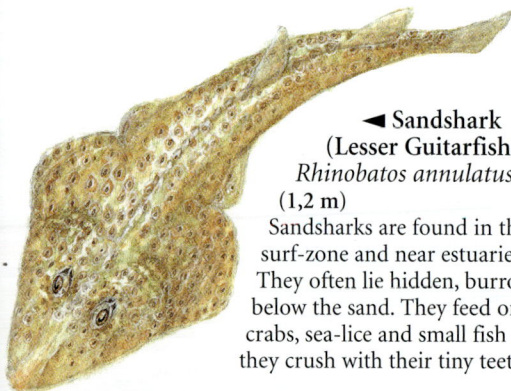

◄ **Sandshark (Lesser Guitarfish)**
Rhinobatos annulatus
(1,2 m)
Sandsharks are found in the surf-zone and near estuaries. They often lie hidden, burrowing below the sand. They feed on crabs, sea-lice and small fish which they crush with their tiny teeth.

Bullray ▼
Pteromylaeus bovinus
(disc width 1,8 m)
Bullrays are found in coastal waters and estuaries. They can be seen on the surface, sometimes leaping from the water. They feed on crabs and mussels, grinding the shells with their flat teeth.

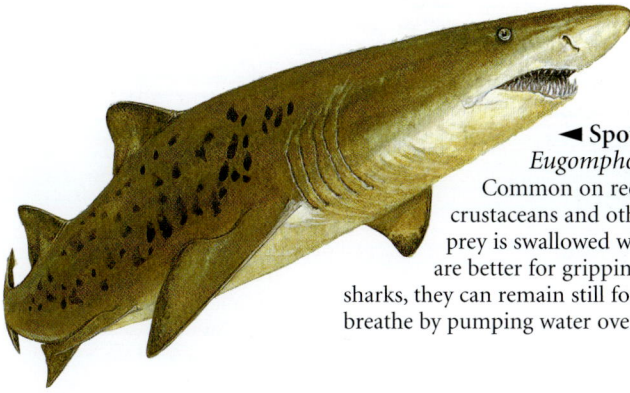

◄ Spotted Ragged-tooth Shark
Eugomphodus taurus (3,2 m)
Common on reefs, they feed on fish,
crustaceans and other smaller sharks. Their
prey is swallowed whole as their smooth teeth
are better for gripping than cutting. Unlike most
sharks, they can remain still for long periods as they can
breathe by pumping water over their gills.

**Great
White
Shark ►**
*Carcharodon
carcharias* (6,4 m)
As super predators, Great
Whites play a vital role in the
food web. They eat fish, other
shark species and marine
mammals such as seals.
Persecuted in the past for
attacking swimmers, divers
and surfers, these sharks are now
protected in South African waters.

▼Smooth Hammerhead Shark
Sphyrna zygaena (3,5 m)
The mouths of hammerheads are on the underside
of the 'hammer' and they have triangular, finely
serrated teeth. They eat bony fish and squid.

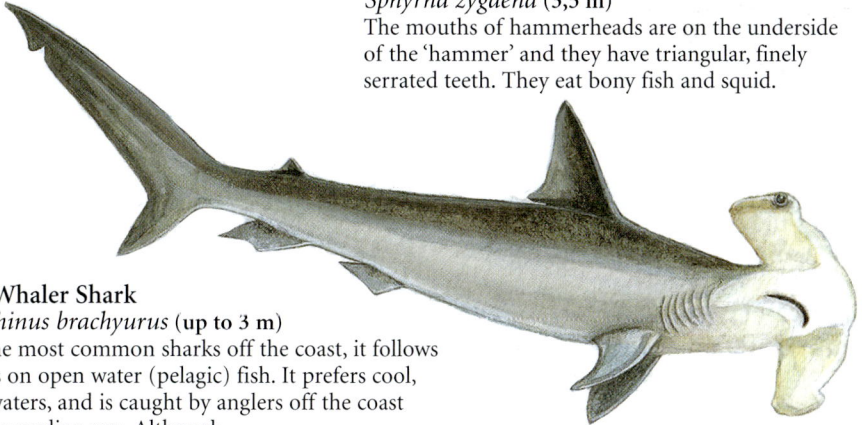

▼Bronze Whaler Shark
Carcharhinus brachyurus (up to 3 m)
One of the most common sharks off the coast, it follows
and preys on open water (pelagic) fish. It prefers cool,
shallow waters, and is caught by anglers off the coast
during the sardine run. Although
a potential danger to man, very
few shark attacks are associated
with this species.

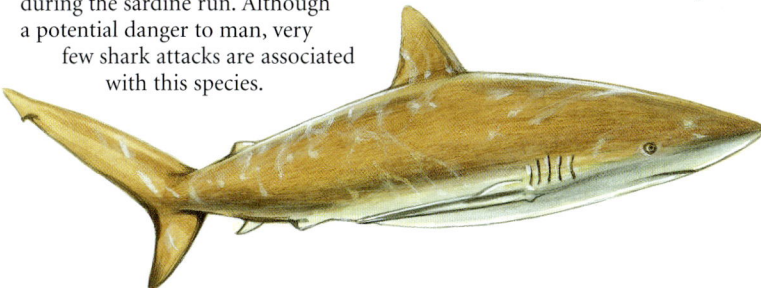

MAINLY MARINE FISH

SHOALING BONY FISH

Bony fish have this name because their skeletons are made up of bone. But they also differ from the cartilaginous fish (see page 42) in having a swim bladder. This allows the fish to maintain neutral buoyancy at different depths without expending too much energy.

The fish illustrated on these pages are those occurring in large shoals in open waters. Shoaling behaviour is a defence against predators which makes an attack on any individual difficult. It also means the predator must spend longer searching for its prey. Many of these fish are coloured dark on the top and pale on the bottom, which provides camouflage to escape predation from above and below.

▼ Cape Anchovy ▲
Engraulis japonicus
(13 cm)
Cape Anchovies are found from the surface of the sea to a depth of 400 m. Being filter-feeders, they sieve planktonic animals from the water. They are an important source of food for marine animals such as dolphins, sharks and seals.

Chokka (Squid) ►
Loligo vulgaris
(20 - 30 cm)
This abundant and significant predator is also an important food source for fish, sharks, sea birds and people who enjoy it as calamari.

◄ Elf (Shad)
Pomatomus saltatrix
(1 m)
Elf are fierce predators with razor-sharp teeth. They feed in shoals on sandy seabeds and reefs eating anchovies, pilchards and pinkies.

Leervis (Garrick) ►
Lichia amia (1,5 m)
These aggressive, swift fish live as predators, forming small hunting shoals in the wave-zone off beaches and rocky points. Elf is their favourite food.

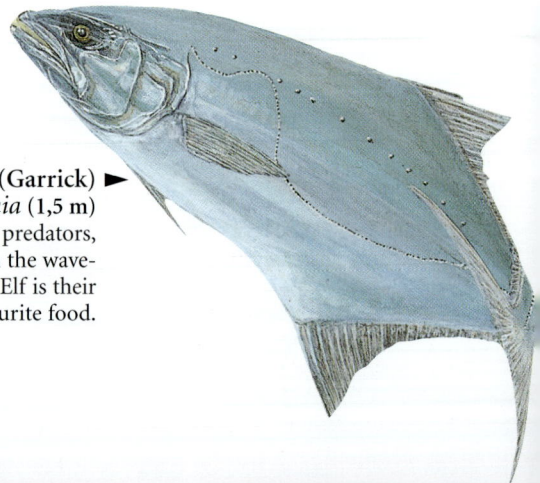

▲ Geelbek ▼

Atractoscion aequidens **(1,2 m)**
Geelbek are common shoaling fish
found in depths of up to 100 m, close to
the bottom of the seabed near steep
ledges or shipwrecks. They eat
maasbanker, mackerel,
pilchard and
sometimes squid.

◄ Pilchard

Sardinops sagax
(30 cm)
These offshore fish form
large shoals and feed on
plankton. Each year sea
currents and gamefish, such
as Tuna, drive them into the surf-zone,
causing the famous 'sardine run'.

◄ ▼Southern Mullet (Harder)

Liza richardsonii
(40 cm)
These fish can be seen off rocky
points and sandy beaches. They feed
on phytoplankton and dead plant
and animal matter.

▲ Cape Yellowtail ►

Seriola lalandi
(1 - 1,5 m)
Common gamefish living
mainly in the Atlantic, they
migrate up the east coast
each winter, following the
'sardine run'. They form
large offshore shoals
up to depths of 50 m.

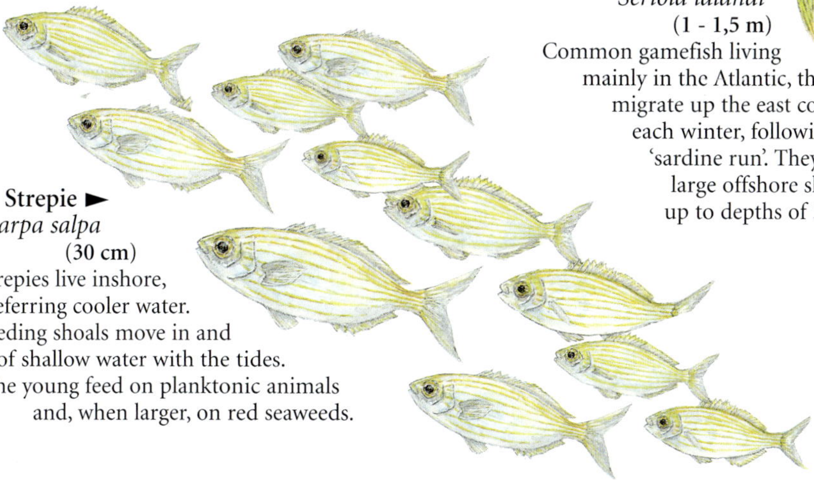

Strepie ►

Sarpa salpa
(30 cm)
Strepies live inshore,
preferring cooler water.
Feeding shoals move in and
out of shallow water with the tides.
The young feed on planktonic animals
and, when larger, on red seaweeds.

45

OTHER BONY FISH

The bony fish illustrated on these pages are those found in deep water, like the Kingklip, but mostly those that live along the rocky reefs and may be seen when snorkelling or scuba diving.

The rocky reefs provide shelter, food and nesting sites for the fish. Caves or seaweed growing on the rocks provide ideal hiding places to escape predation, or places of ambush.

◄ **Blacktail (Dassie)**
Diplodus sargus capensis
(40 cm)
Blacktail like turbulent water and rocky shores, and move in and out with the tides in small shoals. Their food includes seaweed, mussels, sponges and red-bait.

◄ **Zebra** ▼ ►
Diplodus cervinus hottentotus
(50 cm)
These fish are found in rocky areas to a depth of 60 m. Adult fish feed on seaweed, small crabs and tube worms.

◄ **Yellowbelly Rockcod**
Epinephelus marginatus **(1,5 m)**
Found near rocky shores and reefs to a depth of 200 m, they feed on small fish and crustaceans, especially crayfish, which they swallow whole.

▼ **Galjoen**
Coracinus capensis **(80 cm)**
Galjoen are found only in southern Africa and are South Africa's national fish. They are found off rocky shores, and feed on red-bait, seaweed, small mussels and barnacles. They are a protected species. The dark colour depicted here is reached after a little time on land; in the sea it is much lighter.

▼ **Spotted Grunter**
Pomadasys commersonni **(80 cm)**
Living in shallow coastal waters and estuaries, Spotted Grunter feed on worms and shellfish. They blow them out of their burrows with a jet of water forced through their mouths.

◄ **Twotone Fingerfin**
*Chirodactylus
brachydactylus*
(40 cm)
These fish are
found only in
the shallow
reefs of southern
Africa. They feed on mouthfuls
of sand, sifting out small crustaceans
and molluscs, before discarding the
sand through their gill openings.

◄ **Doublesash
Butterflyfish**
Chaetodon marleyi
(10 - 20 cm)
Usually found in pairs,
the adult fish prefer rocky
or coral reefs which range
in depth from 1 - 120 m. They eat a
variety of food including small
invertebrates and seaweed.

▲ **Red Roman** ►
Chrysoblephus laticeps
(30 - 50 cm)
Red Romans are offshore reef
fish found in depths of up to
100 m. They feed on
crustaceans, worms, sea
urchins and other
invertebrates.

Evileyed Puffer (Blaasop) ▼
Amblyrhynchotes honckenii (30 cm)
These spiny fish often lie buried in
sand with only their eyes
protruding, ready to
ambush prey such as
small crabs and slow-
swimming fish. Their
flesh is poisonous to eat.

Kingklip ▼
Genypterus capensis (1,5 m)
Kingklip live on the bottom of the sea around
offshore banks between depths of
50 - 500 m. They feed on fish and
invertebrates, and are one of
South Africa's most
eaten fish.

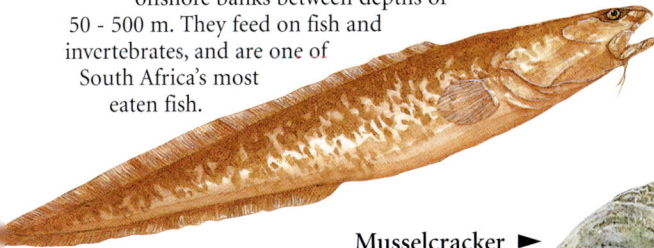

Musselcracker ►
Sparodon durbanensis (1,2 m)
Musselcrackers are large fish found
along rocky shores and shallow
reefs. They like to feed on mussels
which they crush with their
powerful jaws and teeth.

47

Mainly Estuarine Fish

Estuaries are ideal 'nursery' areas for many fish species. They are calm, rich in food, and have few marine predators. However, the eggs and larvae of many estuarine species cannot cope with the constant changes in saltiness, muddiness and temperature, and the irregular movements of the water. The adults usually leave the estuary to spawn (lay their eggs) in a more stable marine environment. Spawning takes place inshore so that the young fish can quickly return to the safe environment of the estuaries.

There is ongoing degradation of estuaries off the southern and eastern Cape coasts. Pollution, over-fishing, erosion, the destruction of salt-marshes and mangroves, and bridge and dam construction can all cause the collapse of estuarine ecosystems, and the loss of many species.

▲ **Kob (Kabeljou)** ▼
Argyrosomus japonicus (2 m)
Kob are shoaling predators that can hunt in dirty water and at night by smelling and sensing the movements of their prey. They eat mainly small fish and crustaceans.

▲ **Cape Sole**
Heteromycteris capensis (15 cm)
Cape Soles are adapted to living in the shallow, sandy areas on the bottom of the sea or estuary. They are found only in southern Africa.

◄ **Knysna Seahorse**
Hippocampus capensis (8 cm)
These exquisite small fish occur only in South Africa in a few southern coast estuaries, particularly Knysna. They are seriously threatened by human development. They use their tails to cling to plants and can change colour.

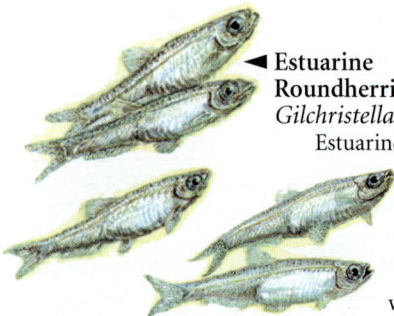

◄ **Estuarine Roundherring**
Gilchristella aestuaria (7 cm)
Estuarine Roundherrings are tiny fish that lack teeth and sieve microscopic animals from the water.

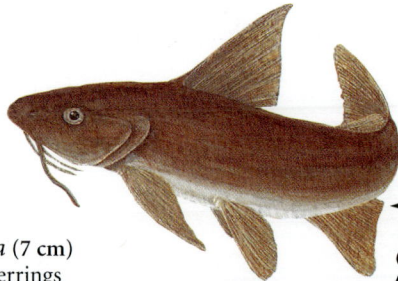

◄ **White Seacatfish**
Galeichthys feliceps (55 cm)
Living in reefs, muddy banks and estuaries, these fish use their barbels to feel for prey on the sea bottom. Males carry the fertilised eggs in their mouths until they hatch.

48

Flathead Mullet ►
Mugil cephalus (80 cm)
Flathead Mullet fish are often
seen jumping out of the water.
They form large shoals and
feed on dead plant material.

White Steenbras ▼
Lithognathus lithognathus (1 m)
Common in shallow water, these fish eat
prawns, shrimps, bloodworms, small
crabs, periwinkles and molluscs. They
blow the prey from their burrows.

**◄ Cape
Stumpnose**
*Rhabdosargus
holubi*
(40 cm)
Stumpnose are
common in shallow coastal
water, and eat plants, molluscs, shrimps and crabs.
They are an important source of food for
subsistence fishermen who live near the estuaries.

Blowing a
prawn hole

◄ Longfin Eel
*Anguilla
mossambica* (1,2 m)
Longfin Eels eat small
invertebrates, crabs, frogs
and fish. After living in freshwater
for 10 years or more, they
return to the Indian
Ocean to breed.

▼ Cape Silverside
Atherina breviceps (11 cm)
Cape Silverside form shoals and feed on
planktonic animals. They breed in
estuaries and can complete their
whole life cycle in
these systems.

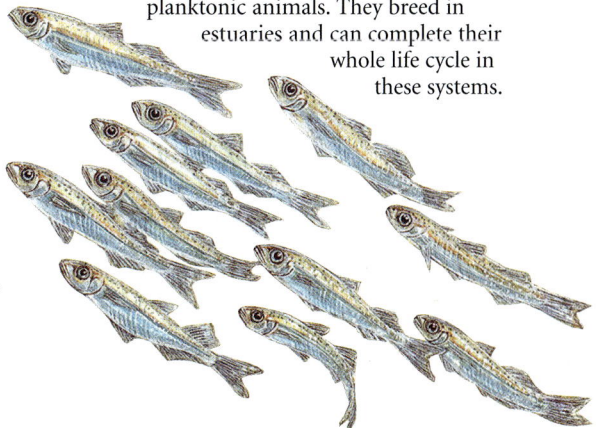

▼ Knysna Sand Goby
Psammogobius knysnaensis (7 cm)
These fish are usually found on sandy banks,
occurring only in southern Africa.
They breed in estuaries and feed
on small invertebrates.

INVERTEBRATES

The invertebrates are a huge, diverse group of animals that lack a supporting spinal column. The ones included here are those found inhabiting the sandy beaches and rocky shores. Unlike the rocky shore inhabitants, the animals using the beaches live beneath the sand and are harder to find.

ROCKY POOLS

Unlike sandy beaches, rocky shores offer shelter and solid foundations on which animals and plants can anchor themselves. Different groups of animals live in different zones up the rocky shore, according to how long they can survive out of the water. For example, limpets prefer the lower shores, barnacles and mussels prefer the mid-shore, and periwinkles, which can survive out of the water for long periods, are found at the top, near the high-tide mark.

The ideal time to study the rocks and pools is when they are exposed at low tide. An overcast day is the perfect opportunity to spend a few hours on the rocks discovering new life at the coast.

▼ Red Starfish
Patiria granifera (**width 80 mm**)
Deep-orange to red in colour, the surface of these starfish resembles overlapping tiles. They feed on dead plant and animal matter.

▼ Spiny Starfish
Marthasterias glacialis (**width 20 cm**)
Spiny Starfish are greedy predators that hunch over mussels prising apart the shells with their feet. The starfish then push out their stomachs to digest them. They also feed on red-bait.

◄ Brown Mussel
Perna perna (**12,5 cm**)
These are edible mussels that secure themselves to rocks by tough threads formed by a gland in the 'foot'. They are filter-feeders, sieving food from the water.

◄ Cushion Star
Patiriella exigua (**width 20 mm**)
Coloured to blend into the rocks, these starfish feed by pushing their stomachs onto the rocks through their centred, underside mouths, where they digest microscopic algae.

Angular Surf Clam ▼
Scissodesma spengleri (**11,3 cm**)
Surf Clams burrow just below the surface of the sand. They are filter-feeders, sucking in water and filtering out food particles as they pass over their gills.

◄ Eye Limpet
Patella oculus (**10 cm**)
Eye Limpets eat algae. Larger ones attack small predators, such as whelks or starfish, by slamming their shells down on them (page 55).

◄ African Periwinkle
Nodilittorina africana (**10 mm**)
Living near the high-water mark, African Periwinkles avoid drying out by closing their shells with a horny trapdoor, or by hanging from rocks on sticky mucus threads (page 55).

Pear Limpet ▼
Patella cochlear (**70 mm**)
Pear Limpets withstand buffeting waves by clinging tightly to the rocks. They scrape the algae off the rocks with long rasping tongues (page 55).

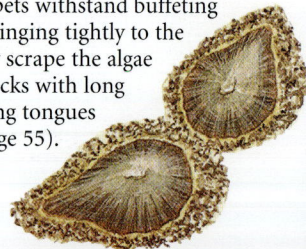

◀ **Red-bait**
Pyura stolonifera (**height 15 cm**)
These sea-squirts live
in crowded groups at
the low-tide zone,
enjoying the
wave action.
They are the
only animals
to make
cellulose in
large quantities.

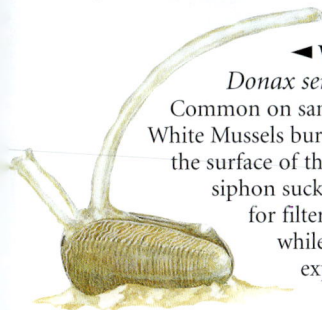

Common Octopus ▼
Octopus vulgaris (**60 cm**)
Octopuses are molluscs that are related
to snails. They can change colour for
protection. They eat crabs, lobsters and
shellfish, and hide in rock cavities.

◀ **White Mussel**
Donax serra (**88 mm**)
Common on sandy beaches,
White Mussels burrow just below
the surface of the sand. One
siphon sucks in water
for filter-feeding,
while the other
expels waste water.

▼ **False Plum Anemone**
Pseudactinia flagellifera
(**width 50 - 100 mm**)
Like other anemones, these animals
cling to rocks with their muscles
and a sticky mucus, while standing
on a fleshy 'foot'. They can move
about slowly, but cannot close up.

◀ **Cape
Urchin**
*Parechinus
angulosus* (**width 60 mm**)
Colourful Cape Urchins feed on
seaweed and microalgae. They use
empty shells as 'hats' for protection
against the sun (page 54).

Plum Anemone ▼
Actinia equina
(**width 20 mm**)
Plum Anemones are
animals that feed on
shrimps and fish which
they catch with the
help of stinging cells in
their tentacles. To survive out of water
they close up, looking like ripe plums.

Cape Rock Oyster ▶
*Striostrea
margaritacea*
(**18 cm**)
Oysters live at the
high-tide level, cemented
to the rocks. They filter-
feed, straining food particles
and micro-organisms from the
water. The Knysna Oyster
Company grows oysters
commercially.

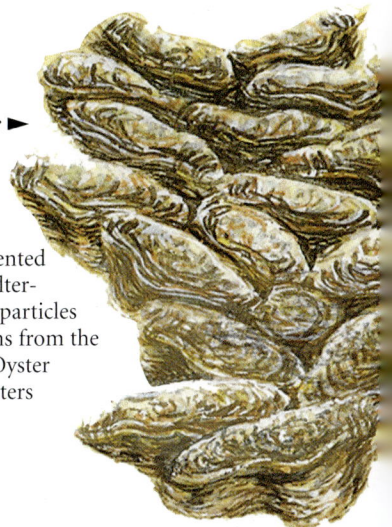

▼ **Three-spot Swimming Crab**
Ovalipes trimaculatus
(**width 40 mm**)
Living beneath the sand in
the surf-zone, they
feed on mussels and
snails. They smash the
shells open with their claws
and then shred the flesh.

51

INVERTEBRATES

SHORELINE, MUD FLATS AND ESTUARIES

Many shoreline sand-dwellers become active at night. Others move up and down the beach with the waves and tides. They depend on food washed up by the waves and blown in by the wind. Their environment is constantly changing.

The mud flats around estuaries are more stable places to live. They support more animals because they are rich in nutrients washed down by the rivers. The animals living here have adapted to coping with changing salt levels in the water.

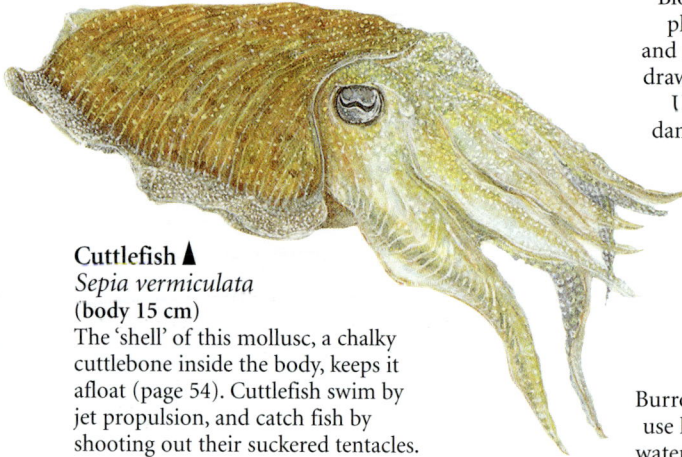

◄ **Horse Mussel**
Atrina squamifera (**39 cm**)
Horse Mussels are fragile animals that lie buried in the sand or mud with the sharp, slightly open back edges of their shells just visible above the surface.

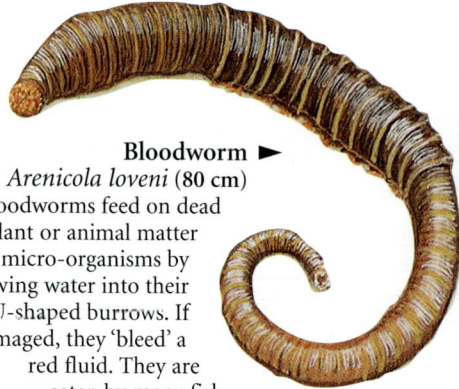

Bloodworm ►
Arenicola loveni (**80 cm**)
Bloodworms feed on dead plant or animal matter and micro-organisms by drawing water into their U-shaped burrows. If damaged, they 'bleed' a red fluid. They are eaten by many fish.

Cuttlefish ▲
Sepia vermiculata
(**body 15 cm**)
The 'shell' of this mollusc, a chalky cuttlebone inside the body, keeps it afloat (page 54). Cuttlefish swim by jet propulsion, and catch fish by shooting out their suckered tentacles.

Pencil-bait ▼
Solen capensis (**16 cm**)
Burrowing into the sand, these molluscs use long siphons to filter food from the water. When their siphons are drawn in, a key-hole shape is left in the sand.

Heart Urchin ►
Echinocardium cordatum
(**40 mm**)
All sea urchins' bodies are protected by a fragile shell with spines. Heart Urchins' mouths have a scoop-like lip for feeding on dead plant and animal matter.

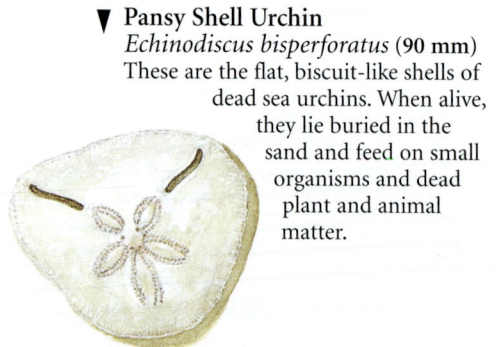

▼ **Pansy Shell Urchin**
Echinodiscus bisperforatus (**90 mm**)
These are the flat, biscuit-like shells of dead sea urchins. When alive, they lie buried in the sand and feed on small organisms and dead plant and animal matter.

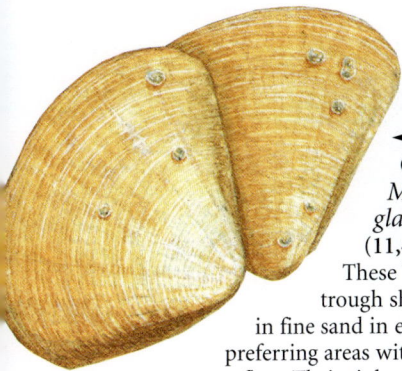

◄ White Clam
Mactra glabrata
(11,4 cm)
These 'smooth trough shells' burrow in fine sand in estuaries, preferring areas with strong water-flow. Their siphons extend above the sand, drawing in water from which they filter food.

Giant Mud Crab ▲
Scylla serrata (width 30 cm)
Amongst the largest swimming crabs, they have powerful nippers and paddle-shaped back legs. They come out of the sand or mud at sunset to feed on molluscs and shellfish.

Common Sand Hermit Crab ►
Diogenes brevirostris
(30 mm)
Living in empty shells, they use their larger left nipper as a door. They are scavengers but can also filter food from the water with feathery 'arms'.

Crown Crab ▼
Hymenosoma orbiculare (15 mm)
Abundant in estuaries, where they live in sandbanks, these pale crabs are mottled by brown microalgae. They feed on small shellfish.

◄ Marsh Crab
Sesarma catenata
(25 mm)
They are common crabs that burrow in sand and mud flats near the high-tide mark. They suck in mud and sand particles, to feed on rotting plant and animal matter.

Estuarine Mudprawn ▼
Upogebia africana
(40 mm)
Living in muddy sand in estuaries, these prawns pump water through their U-shaped burrows, filtering out food particles. Fishermen collect them for bait.

▲ Sand Prawn
Callianassa kraussi (60 mm)
Found in estuaries where the water current is stronger, Sand Prawns live in deep burrows and feed by sifting the sand for plant and animal matter.

53

INVERTEBRATES

ALONG THE DRIFTLINE

The driftline is the only part of the beach that is reached by waves at high tide. It is a fascinating place to wander and discover the new treasures brought out by the sea.

As in all natural systems, plants and animals are continuously dying, while new ones are born to take their place in the life cycle. Crabs and other scavengers may be spotted moving amongst the debris. They feed on the dead matter, thereby recycling nutrients back into the system.

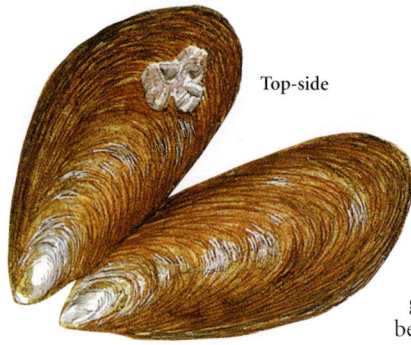

Top-side

◄ **Brown Mussel**
Perna perna (12,5 cm)
The taller, narrower shells are from faster growing mussels, from below the tidal-zone. The smaller, triangular shells are from crowded, intertidal beds of mussels (page 51).

Under-side

▲ **Horn-eyed Ghost Crab**
Ocypode ceratophthalmus
(width 40 mm)
Ghost Crabs dig very deep holes high up on sheltered beaches. They come out at low tide to scavenge on dead animals and plants.

◄ **Cuttlefish/Cuttlebone**
(30 - 170 mm)
This is the internal chalky plate which once supported a cuttlefish (page 52) and allowed it to control its buoyancy. They are very light and are often washed ashore after the animals die.

◄ **Cape Urchin**
Parechinus angulosus
(60 mm)
These are the left-over shells of the sea urchin (page 51).

◄ **Common Shore Crab
(Rocky Shore Crab)**
Cyclograpsus punctatus
(width 30 mm)
Common, but seldom seen, these crabs hide under stones high up the beach. They scavenge at night during low tide, feeding mostly on seaweed, but also on dead animals.

◄ **Variegated Topshell ▼**
Oxystele variegata
(25 mm)
These winkles use rough file-like 'tongues' to scrape algae off rocks. When young, they live lower down on rocky shores, moving up the beach as they get bigger.

Under-side

Top-side

Top-side

Under-side

Pink-lipped Topshell ▲ ►
Oxystele sinensis (45 mm)
These winkles feed on algae and live along rocky shores. They look like spinning tops.

Under-side

Top-side

Top-side

Under-side

▲ Duck's Foot Limpet
Patella longicosta (70 mm)
Also called the 'Long-spined Limpets',
the young live on other shells, and then
move to the rocks where they look
after algal 'gardens'.

▲ Eye Limpet
Patella oculus (10 cm)
Eye Limpets change from male
to female after the first year
(page 50).

Under-side

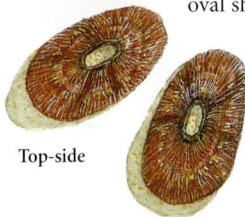

▼ Key-hole Limpet
Dendrofissurella scutellum
(40 mm)
Key-hole Limpets have flat,
oval shells with a central
hole through which
the animals expel
their waste.

Top-side

Pink-rayed Limpet ▼
Patella miniata (80 mm)
Living on rocky shores, they
scrape coralline algae off
the rocks.
Like other
limpets,
they
return to
their home
patch after
feeding.

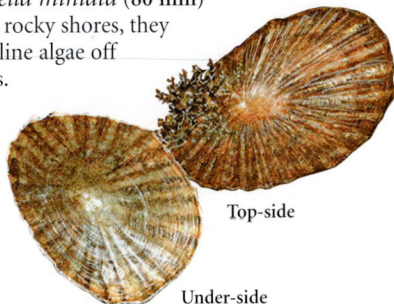

Top-side

Under-side

Pear Limpet ▼
Patella cochlear
(70 mm)
The inner surface of
these shells is smooth and
white, tinged with blue.
There is a U-shaped scar
where the animal's muscle
was attached (page 50).

Under-side

Top-side

▼ Cape False Limpet
Siphonaria capensis (25 mm)
Unlike other limpets, False Limpets
breathe air at low tide
through their siphons.
When under water,
they use their gills
to breathe. They
produce a toxic
mucus that repels
predators.

Top-side

Under-side

Top-side

▼African
Periwinkle ►
*Nodilittorina africana
knysnaensis* (10 mm)
These periwinkles vary in
colour, from flecked-brown to
almost black
(page 50).

Under-side

Mermaid's Purse ▼
(50 - 100 mm)
This is an egg case produced by small
sharks such as the Shyshark. The curly
tendrils attach the case to seaweed while
the fish develops.

INVERTEBRATES

MORE DRIFTLINE TREASURES

Bits and pieces of plant and animal skeletons, both vertebrate and invertebrate, are scattered among the debris of the driftline as the sea continually tosses their remains onto the shore with every high tide. Look out for Plough Snails which suddenly emerge out of the sand at the first scent of food. The shells are the dead remains of animals that can be found living on the rocks.

◄ **Goose Barnacle**
Lepas spp.
(30 mm)
At sea, these crustaceans cluster on bits of wood or other objects. They cannot move around, and they feed by waving feathery legs in the water to trap food particles.

Screw Shell ▼
Turritella carinifera
(70 mm)
Screw Shells are found under rocks lying on the sand. These animals are filter-feeders.

▲ **Venus Ear (Siffie/Abalone)**
Haliotis spadicea **(80 mm)**
The inside of this beautiful shell is mother-of-pearl. Venus Ears live in rocky crevices and amongst Red-bait (page 51), feeding on red algae.

Ram's Horn Shell ▼
Spirula spirula **(25 mm)**
These are the internal shells of small squid-like animals that float in the deep sea and are rarely seen alive.

Top-side

◄ **Slipper Limpet**
Crepidula porcellana **(15 mm)**
The limpet larvae settle and grow on shells of other molluscs, often forming stacks on top of one another. They change sex as they mature. They are filter-feeders.

Under-side

▼ **Root-mouthed Jellyfish**
Rhizostoma spp. **(width 30 cm)**
The illustration shows a broken piece of the dead jellyfish with Plough Snails feeding. It is the largest species of jellyfish, but does not have stinging tentacles for catching food. Instead, these animals filter-feed on microscopic animals.

▼ **Plough Snail** ▼
Bullia digitalis **(60 mm)**
When the tide starts to rise, this snail comes out of the sand, spreads its large 'foot' like a sail, and surfs up the beach to feed on dead animals.

Smooth Turban Shell ▶

Turbo cidaris cidaris (**30 mm**)
These snails live in rock pools or under boulders, along the mid-shore. They eat plants.

◀ **Mottled Necklace Shell**

Natica tecta (**41 mm**)
The snails feed on mussels. They secrete acids to drill holes into the shells of their prey.

Operculum (shell lid)

▲ **Alikreukel (Giant Periwinkle)**

Turbo sarmaticus (**10 cm**)
These molluscs can close their shells using a white 'lid' which prevents water-loss. They live in rock pools and feed on algae at night.

Furry-ridged Triton ▼

Cymatium cutaceum africanum (**50 mm**)
The shell shapes are variable. When alive, these whelk shells are coated with a brown 'fur', and are often found amongst Red-bait (page 51) on which they may feed.

Striped Burnupena ▶

Burnupena pubescens (**50 mm**)
These whelks live in the subtidal-zone. They eat wounded or dead animals which they find by detecting the scent carried in water currents.

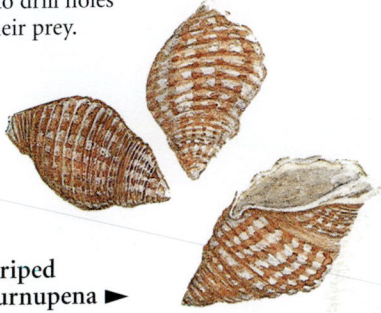

◀ **Bluebottle**

Physalia physalia (float 50 mm long, tentacles 10 m or 30 cm when contracted)
Each Bluebottle is a colony of four independent specialised animals living together. They float on the surface of the open sea, relying on winds and currents to move them around. Their long tentacles, which are used to catch prey, shoot out stinging barbs when touched.

Bubble-raft Shell ▶

Janthina janthina (**34 mm**)
Bubble-rafts are the shells of violet snails that drift around the open sea, held up by a float of bubbles. They feed on bluebottles.

▼ **Beach Hopper (Sand Hopper)**

Talorchestia capensis (**10 - 12 mm**)
Beach Hoppers are crustaceans that feed on seaweed at night. They are often found under driftwood and become very active when disturbed.

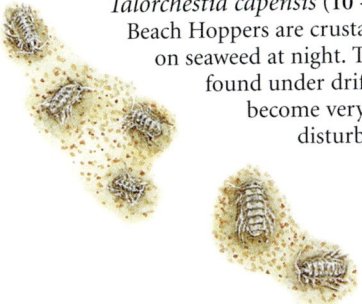

Tick Shell ▼

Nassarius kraussianus (**7 - 10 mm**)
These tiny snails live in mud banks and feed on small bivalves or dead animal and plant matter. They sense their food by holding their siphons erect, like an elephant's trunk.

Top-side

Under-side

57

PLANTS AND INSECTS

The climate and geology of an area are the main factors determining the vegetation types and plant diversity occurring there. The plain between the coast and the mountain slopes, stretching from George to Tsitsikamma, enjoys high year-round rainfall that allows the growth of huge trees in indigenous forests. Near the coast and on the mountains, conditions are not favourable for closed canopy, large tree-growth. Here, Cape fynbos, which is adapted to the harsher conditions, thrives. Numerous rivers flow from the mountains towards the sea, and provide additional habitats. These habitats harbour microhabitats, which offer a great variety of food shelter and breeding sites for animals.

A number of insects have been illustrated with the plants. They all interact with the plants in some way, and are associated with certain habitat types.

Sizes given refer to the height of the average adult plant, to the wingspan of butterflies or to the body length of other insects. Where appropriate the month in which these plants flower is given. The national tree number is also given after the size of each species.

The King Protea, South Africa's national flower, in all its glorious majesty

FORESTS

South Africa's dry climate means that less than 0,5% of the country is covered in indigenous forests. The magnificent forests of the Knysna-Tsitsikamma region are amongst our finest. They are a breathtakingly beautiful, living monument to millions of years of natural history. They show how the Coastal Plain eco-system looked and functioned before urbanisation and industrialisation.

THE BIGGER TREES

Many of the trees, particularly yellowwoods, ironwood and stinkwood grow to a massive size, even by world standards. Because of this, their timber has been important in shaping the human history of the southern Cape, and relatively few of the huge trees remain today. However a number of impressive yellowwoods can be seen driving along the N2 between Nature's Valley and Storms River, where there is a patch of very valuable indigenous forest.

It is important to be pro-active in the protection of precious, irreplaceable forest patches. No single reason for human advancement can possibly, long-term, overshadow the need to keep the very little forest we have left.

◄▼ **Cape-chestnut**
Calodendrum capense
Oct - Dec
(7 - 20 m) 256
Evergreen
This tree has smooth, grey bark with white and orange patches, and large, dark, strong-smelling leaves. Its large flowers vary from white to pale-pink. The seeds are in woody, knobbly capsules. It grows along the coastal strip, in river valleys and in forests.

▼ **Broom-cluster Fig** ►
Ficus sur
Sep - Mar (15 - 25 m)
50 Semi-deciduous
This distinctive fig, well-named for its unusual bunches of fruit, naturally occurs in protected ravines near the coast. It was a favoured species for making fire by frictioning two "fire sticks" – one of its earliest names.

◄ **Forest Tree Fern** ▼
Cyathea capensis
No flowers (5 m) 2 Evergreen
The trunk is covered with blackish leaf-stubs and scales. The large leaves can be up to 3 metres long. It grows in moist conditions and in high forests. The Common Tree Fern is similar, and is often found on forest edges and along grassy mountain streams.

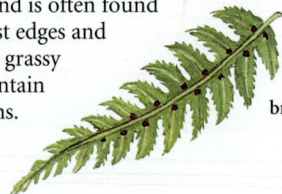

Under-side of leaf-frond, showing brown spores

Cicada ▼
Family Cicadidac (45 mm)
With their piercing mouth parts, these insects feed on tree juices (sap). The shrill, droning noise often heard from trees and bushes is made by male cicadas. Females lay eggs in slits in tree bark.

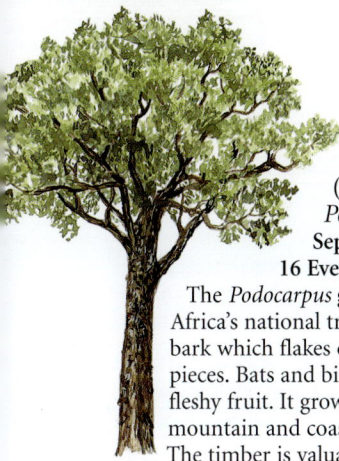

◀ ▼ **Small-leaved
Yellowwood
(Outeniqua Yellowwood)**
Podocarpus falcatus
Sep - May (20 - 60 m)
16 Evergreen
The *Podocarpus* genus is South
Africa's national tree. It has smooth
bark which flakes off in irregular
pieces. Bats and birds eat its yellow,
fleshy fruit. It grows in ravines and in
mountain and coastal, swamp forests.
The timber is valuable, and in the past,
the trunks were used for ship masts.

◀ **Broad-leaved
Yellowwood ▲
(Real Yellowwood)**
Podocarpus latifolius
Jul - Sep (20 - 30 m)
18 Evergreen
The bark varies from yellow-
brown to dark-brown and peels
off in long strips. The cones are
pink on male trees, and bright red
on female trees. The pale-yellow
timber has always been highly valued,
especially as flooring in old
Cape houses.

◀ **Small
Ironwood ▶**
Olea capensis
Aug - Feb (10 - 40 m)
618 Deciduous
The bark darkens with age and, if
damaged, it 'bleeds' a slimy, black gum.
It has very small, white or cream,
scented flowers, and the olive-like
purple fruit is eaten by many birds and
animals. In the past, this hard, grained wood
was used for railway sleepers.

Stinkwood ▼ ▶
Ocotea bullata
Dec - Feb (8 - 30 m)
118 Evergreen
When young, the bark of this
tree is smooth with a
variety of coloured
patches. Older trees
have rougher grey-
brown bark. Its large,
oblong leaves have
'blisters' at their base,
and smell strongly if crushed.
The freshly cut wood has an
unpleasant smell. However,
its beautiful timber is often
used to make furniture.

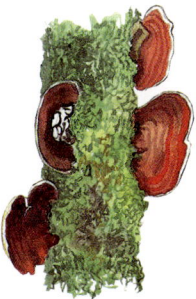

◀ **Bracket Fungus**
(many species commonly known under the
name) (size varies)
This is generally known as Bracket Fungi because
the fruit-body projects like a bracket from either
dead wood, branches or tree trunks. It plays an
integral part in the decomposition of wood.

FORESTS

MORE BIG TREES

From the early 1800s, trees were used for building ships, houses and furniture, and for fuel. It soon became necessary to protect the forests legally. Although much of the wood-supply now comes from commercial plantations, indigenous forests still need protection from human activities, such as building, farming and even recreation. However, hiking, walking, cycling, horse riding, birding, tree spotting, swimming and picnicking in our forests are a wonderful way to spend time in the Garden Route.

▲ **Common Forest Grape** ▼
Rhoicissus tomentosa
Oct - Dec Deciduous (3 - 7 m as a small tree; as a climber can reach the top of 20 m high trees) 456.5
The leaves are dark-green above and hairy below. Young vines attach themselves to small trees, and as the trees grow they are lifted up into the forest canopy. Flowers grow in dense heads and are small, creamy-green. Birds eat the purple fruit (Jan - Apr).

◄ **Western Keurboom** ▼
Virgilia oroboides Aug - Sep or Dec - Jan (10 m) 221 Deciduous
It has brown-grey, smooth bark and leaves with small leaflets – glossy green above and hairy below. Sprays of pink-mauve flowers change to long, flat, brown, velvety pods. It grows in coastal forest edges and river valleys.

◄ ▼ **Cape-beech**
Rapanea melanaphloes
Jun - Dec (5 - 20 m) 578 Evergreen
This can be relatively easy to identify because younger stems and branches are pale grey, and covered with small, flat knobs, resembling ostrich skin. It is widespread in mountain ranges and forests in eastern South Africa, and from Cape Town to the Limpopo.

▼ **Large-leaved Cape-ash**
Ekebergia capensis
Sep - Nov (10 - 30 m) 298 Evergreen
Although relatively rare, growing naturally as far south as the Garden Route, it is planted extensively in all the major towns as a street and garden tree. Its unusual-shaped, asymmetrical, compound leaves and bunched, red, berry-like fruit make it easily confused with Wild-plum (*Harpephyllum caffrum*).

White-alder ►
Platylophus trifoliatus
Dec (25 m) 141
Evergreen

Three of these four trees (**White-alder**, **White-ironwood** and **Red Currant-rhus**) have **three-leaflet compound leaves**. The **Red-alder** has 3 - 5 pairs of leaflets and an end leaflet. They are all beautiful trees, worth finding, and are fairly common along the Garden Route. The Red Currant-rhus is likely to be found at forest margins as a pioneer plant, or in gardens, in both instances growing from bird droppings. White-ironwood is in similar forest habitat, and the strong lemon smell from crushed leaves is diagnostic. Both White-alder and Red-alder need high levels of moisture, and particularly the Red-alder is found leaning over streams and rivers. The White-alder is endemic, and makes a wonderful honey that is worth searching for at local farm stalls.

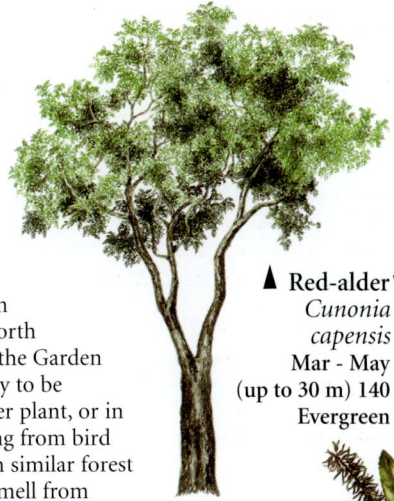

▲ **Red-alder** ▼
Cunonia capensis
Mar - May
(up to 30 m) 140
Evergreen

▼ **Red Currant-rhus** ▼
Rhus chirindensis
Nov - Dec (6 - 10 m)
380 Evergreen

White-ironwood ▲
Vepris lanceolata
Dec - Mar
(15 m) 261
Evergreen

Assegai ▼
Curtisia dentata
Oct - Mar (15 m) 570 Evergreen
The first reference to this tree in the Cape is in a forest survey of 1662. There the name used is the same as that used for spears, by Jan van Riebeeck in 1652, "*hassegaayen*". From the earliest days timber was prized by colonists for building and wagon-making, as well as the leaves for tanning. It is no wonder that many of the older, larger trees were destroyed. To find this tree, keep a look out for the spectacularly rigid, glossy, spikily serrated leaves on lower-level shoots.

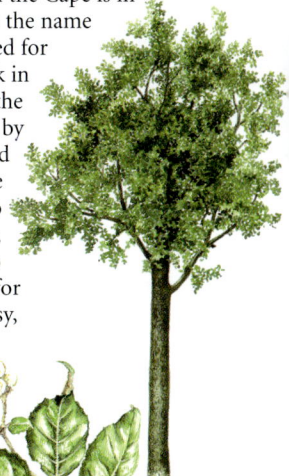

◄ **Forest Nuxia** ▼
(**Forest Elder**)
Nuxia floribunda
May - Aug
(3 - 10 m) 634 Evergreen
The bark of this small tree is pale-grey, smooth and powdery. It bears sprays of tiny, fragrant, cream-white flowers, and has small egg-shaped, creamy-brown fruit which, when mature, split into four, releasing the fine seed (Jun - Oct). It grows in evergreen forests and forest edges. The pale-yellow wood is hard and heavy, and it was used to make wagons.

FORESTS

BUSHES AND FLOWERING PLANTS

In many of the more open patches, where old trees have fallen, sunlight sprinkles across the lower layers, and allows bushes and flowering plants to thrive. Here birding is more likely to be successful too.

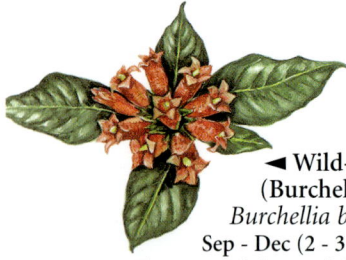

◄ **Tree-fuchsia** ▼
Halleria lucida
May - Dec
(2 - 3 m) 670 Evergreen

A shrub or small tree, occasionally much larger, the Tree-fuchsia occurs in coastal scrub, forest and rocky mountain slopes. The nectar and fruit are extremely attractive to a wide variety of birds such as sunbirds and bulbuls.

◄ **Wild-pomegranate** ▼
(Burchellia)
Burchellia bubalina
Sep - Dec (2 - 3 m) 688 Evergreen

The unusual shape of the flowers and fruit make this small tree a tree-spotters favourite, and both flowers and fruit attract birds, and therefore birders! Both the botanical name *bubalina* (from the latin *bubalus* - buffalo) and an original Afrikaans name, Buffelshoring, describe the twisted calyx horns on the fruit.

Poison Star-apple ▲
Diospyros dicrophyllua
Nov - Mar (2 - 3 m)
603 Evergreen

This large bush or small tree is in the same family as the very large, well-loved Lowveld tree, Jackal-berry (*Diospyros mespiliformis*). Their leaves and fruit are similar. Again the Afrikaans name 'Tolbos' is interesting, referring to the way fruit can spin on the ground, like a top, if it is kicked. It is the fruit that is poisonous.

◄ **Candlewood** ▼
(Cherrywood)
Pterocelastrus tricuspidatus
Jul - Nov (7 - 25 m)
409 Evergreen

Often seen growing as a shrub, this tree has smooth, dark-brown bark, and thick, leathery, shiny leaves. The young branches, leaves and leaf-stalks are pink to red. Its fragrant flowers are creamy-white and its lobed, 'winged' fruit is bright-yellow. It is often found in dune-scrub, as well as in dry to medium-moist forests.

◄ **Black Witch-hazel** ►
Trichocladus crinitus
Apr - Aug (3 - 4 m) 142
Evergreen

This shrub or small tree has smooth bark, and brown hairs on the stems and under-surface of the leaves. It has spider-like heads of cream-green, yellow or orange flowers. The fruit forms clusters of hairy, brown-red capsules. It is common in medium-moist forests, and its wood is white and very hard.

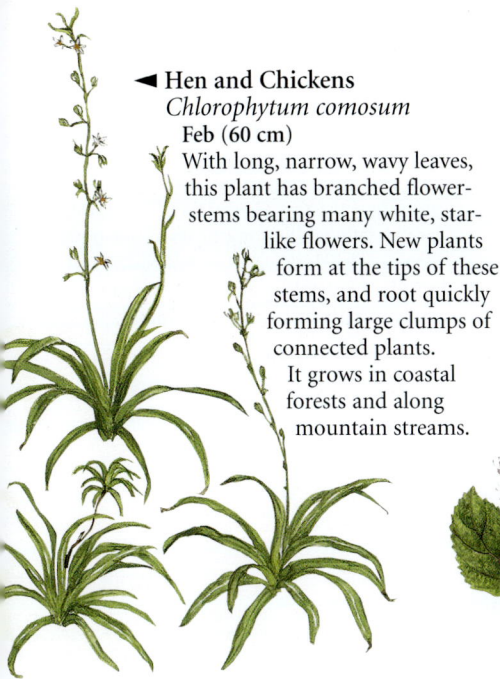

◄ Hen and Chickens
Chlorophytum comosum
Feb (60 cm)
With long, narrow, wavy leaves, this plant has branched flower-stems bearing many white, star-like flowers. New plants form at the tips of these stems, and root quickly forming large clumps of connected plants. It grows in coastal forests and along mountain streams.

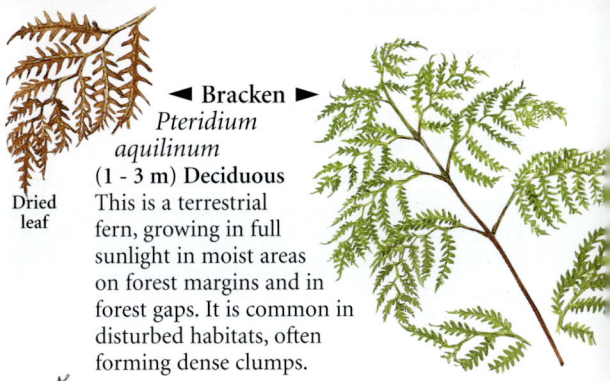

◄ Bracken ►
Pteridium aquilinum
(1 - 3 m) Deciduous
This is a terrestrial fern, growing in full sunlight in moist areas on forest margins and in forest gaps. It is common in disturbed habitats, often forming dense clumps.

Dried leaf

◄ Spur Flower
Plectranthus ecklonii
Mar - May (1,2 - 2 m)
The Spur Flower is a large straggling shrub with strong-smelling leaves and stems. The flowers form a series of pale and dark purple circular sprays. It prefers moist places and deep shade.

◄ Mosquito
Family Culicidae
(4 - 10 mm)
Mosquitoes are most active at night, and feed on nectar and the juice of ripe fruits. Females have piercing mouth-parts, and also feed on blood. Males can be identified by their feathery antennae. Garden Route mosquitoes do not transmit malaria.

Twin Sisters (Cape Primrose) ►
Streptocarpus rexii
Nov - Aug (12 - 24 cm)
The thick, wrinkled, velvety leaves of this plant lie flat on the ground. It has mauve to dark-purple flowers, and its seed-pods split in a spiral. It is found along shady forest streams.

◄ Blue Lily (Agapanthus)
Agapanthus praecox
Dec - Apr
(40 - 60 cm)
This species has long, narrow, dark-green leaves and blue to purple, trumpet-shaped flowers that grow in a round ball at the end of the long stem. It is often found growing in clumps on sea cliffs and in coastal forests.

Arum Lily ▼
Zantedeschia aethiopica
Mainly Sep - Dec (1,5 m)
Arum Lilies have fleshy stalks and glossy, pointed leaves. The flowers are usually creamy-white, with a single folded petal around a bright yellow rod. They grow well in damp ground, often in large clusters.

65

FYNBOS

Fynbos grows in the Cape Floral Kingdom, the smallest of the world's six floral kingdoms, but with the greatest diversity of plant species. Fire plays an important role in driving the system and maintaining this great diversity.

INDICATOR SPECIES

The Ericas, Restios and Proteas illustrated on this page are all indicator species of Cape fynbos. Fynbos grows on nutrient-poor, acidic soils. It is characterised by its short scrubby appearance (average 1 - 2 metres). The word fynbos comes from the Dutch description of the small, fine-leaved plants that are common.

A major threat to fynbos is the spread of alien plants such as Hakea, Black Wattle and pine trees. Other threats include too many fires, often in the wrong season, the planting of large areas of trees for commercial use, and the development of housing estates and farms. The conservation of fynbos is a national priority.

◄ **Ker Ker (Raasheide)**
Erica imbricata July - Dec (30 - 50 cm)
This upright shrublet grows on sandy flats, hills and mountain slopes, and is more abundant west of Mossel Bay. The flowers are usually white, sometimes a dull-pink or red. The dark stamens protrude from inside the petals, giving this Erica a very distinctive, attractive appearance.

Hairy Erica ►
Erica hispidula
Oct - Dec (50 - 80 cm)
This small shrub is very abundant on hills and mountains slopes, and common in sandy, dry places but will grow in damp areas. It is wind- not animal-pollinated. Not needing to attract birds or insects, the flowers are small and inconspicuous. Clouds of pollen may be lifted when walking through stands in full bloom.

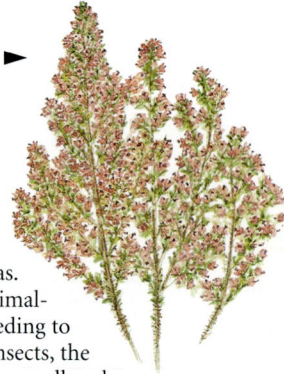

◄ **Common Heath**
Erica sparsa
Dec - Apr (up to 2 m)
Common Heath has small, bell-shaped, pale-pink flowers. It grows on southern slopes of coastal mountains.

◄ **Vlakte Heath**
Erica coccinea
Apr - Dec (0,6 - 1 m)
Vlakte Heath is very common on the southern slopes of the Outeniqua and Tsitsikamma mountains. The flowers are densely packed, coloured green, yellow or red. It is found in moist, sandy places on hills and mountains. The small leaves are grouped in tufts up the branches.

Erica ►
Erica versicolor
Apr - Jun (1 m)
The small flowers on this tall bush vary in colour according to where they grow. One form has flowers which are tube-shaped, red at the base with green-white tips. Sunbirds visit the bush to eat the nectar from the flowers. It grows on lower mountain slopes.

King Protea ▶
(Giant Protea)
Protea cynaroides
All year round
(0,3 - 2 m)
This is South Africa's
national flower. The large
flowers (up to 30 cm across)
vary from cone-shaped to
bowl-shaped, and are various shades
of pink. After a fire the plant
quickly re-grows from its thick,
underground stems.

◀ Cape Scarab
Beetle ▶
Trichostetha
fasicularis (10 - 20 mm)
These brightly coloured
beetles are strong
flyers. Adults are
often found looking
for nectar in
Protea flowers,
while the larvae
feed on decaying
vegetable matter.

(F)

Restios
Family Restionaceae
With over 300 species, Restios are
common in, as well as indicators of,
fynbos. Similar in appearance to grasses,
these reed-like plants in fact
belong to a different plant family.
Restios actually take the place of
true grasses in fynbos vegetation,
and have an important function as
ground cover. Interestingly, Restios
are unisexual, the male and
female being on different plants.
Like all fynbos vegetation, they
are able to survive fires in many
different ways. They are widely
used for thatching.

Sugarbush ▶
(Suikerbossie)
Protea repens
All year round (4,5 m)
The leaves of this Protea are
leathery, and the flowers
vary from white to dark-
pink and have sticky
'scales'. The seeds are
like upside-down ice-
cream cones. It flowers
mainly May - Oct in the west,
Sep - Mar in the eastern regions.
The flowers produce a lot of nectar
which, in the 19th Century, was collected
and boiled to make cough medicine.

(M)

◀ Elegant Restio
Elegia racemosa
Dec - Mar (up to 6 cm)

▼ Wart-stem
Pincushion
Leucospermum
cuneiforme
Sep - Nov
(1,5 m)
This Protea has
toothed leaves at the
top, and 'warts' at the base
of its stems. The flowers can
be yellow, red or orange,
depending on the area in
which they grow.

Thatching Reed ▶
Thamnochortus
erectus

(M)

◀ Geelbos ▶
(Sunshine Cone Bush)
Leucadendron salignum
Jul - Sep (1 - 2 m)
The young leaves are lemon-yellow,
becoming darker green with red
margins and tips. These plants often
cover large areas of mountain slopes
and flats. The flowers are on woody
cones, with the female and male
flowers on separate plants. The winged
seeds stay in woody cones on the plant
until after a fire.

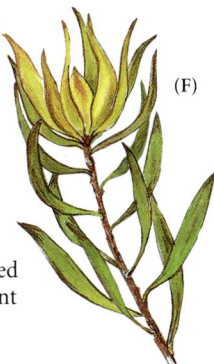

(F)

Pugnaceous Ants ▶
Anoplolepis custodiens
These ants bury fynbos
seeds so that the seeds
are able to germinate
successfully after fire.

67

Fynbos

Other Flowering Plants

An important but often inconspicuous component of fynbos are plants with bulbs. The bulbs, hidden under the soil, go unnoticed until they receive a particular environmental cue, such as rain or fire. The flowers that emerge are often the most beautiful and spectacular found in the fynbos. The bulbs of orchid species are much sought-after by collectors, and have become rare as a result.

Dune Daisy ►
Felicia echinata
Flowers most of the year (60 cm)
The Dune Daisy is a small shrub seen along the roads and on dunes.

▼ Citrus Swallowtail ►
(Christmas Butterfly)
Papilio demodocus
Visible all year (7 - 9 cm)
These insects are most common during the summer, particularly in December. The caterpillars feed on the leaves of various plants.

Caterpillar stage

◄ Spider Orchid
Bartholina ethelae
Oct - Jan (8 - 15 m)
The small, circular leaf of this plant grows flat on the ground, and it has one stem with a purple flower. It is a rare plant and grows in damp, shady places.

▼ Green Wood-orchid ►
Bonatea speciosa
Oct - Nov (90 cm)
Wavy-edged, pointed leaves enclose the stem of this orchid which grows in the semi-shade of coastal bush and forest edges. It is pollinated by the Hawk Moth which is attracted to its fragrant green and white flowers.

Convolvulus Hawk Moth ▲
Agrius convolvuli
Visible at night (8 cm)
These large moths are often seen hovering over flowers, feeding on nectar. When not feeding, they coil their long tongues beneath their heads.

Praying Mantis ►
Sphodiomantis gastica (20 - 85 mm)
Varying greatly in shape and colour, these insects can look like leaves, grass, flowers or tree bark. They catch insects with their front legs which are held in a 'praying' position.

◄ Duine-aandblom ▼
Freesia alba
Aug - Nov (15 - 30 cm)
This thin-leaved plant has very fragrant, cream-yellow flowers tinged with purple. It grows in dune-scrub and even in pure sand at the edge of freshwater lakes.

◄ Golden Orchid
Disa cornuta
Sep - Feb (30 - 50 cm)
Found from Humansdorp to Mossel Bay, the Golden Orchid grows in full sunlight, on mountains and sandy places. The outer hood is a dull purple but it sparkles golden in the sunlight. It is densely leafy, with reddish-purple spots at the base of the leaves.

Blue Disa ►
Disa graminifolia
Mar - Apr (30 - 60 cm)
When hiking in the Outeniqua Mountains, look out for the striking, bright blue flowers. The Blue Disa is widespread but not very common. It prefers higher mountain slopes, usually on rocky soils.

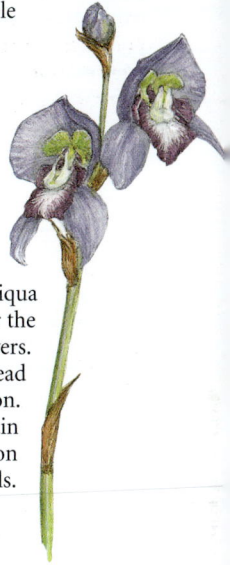

◄ Cluster Disa
Disa ferruginea
Feb - Apr (20 - 50 cm)
The Cluster Disa is found especially in the Montagu and Robinson Pass areas. Although it does not produce its own nectar, it mimics other flower species that do, and is pollinated by a specialised butterfly. This grass-like orchid grows on rocks in the cloud belt of the Cape mountains. The bright red-orange flowers appear before leaves. It is a protected flower.

Suurkanol ►
Chasmanthe aethiopica
May - Jun (60 cm)
Many scarlet flowers grow on one side of the flowering stem. Its leaves grow in downward rows around the stem, and its seeds are bright orange. In shady embankments it can form large colonies, growing from the previous year's 'bulb' and long, underground shoots.

Watsonia ▼
Watsonia fourcadei
Nov (1,2 m)
The long narrow leaves of this plant form a fan around its base, and the flower-stem bears white or pink flowers. Growing on mountain foothills, the flowers are particularly abundant when good rain follows a bush-fire.

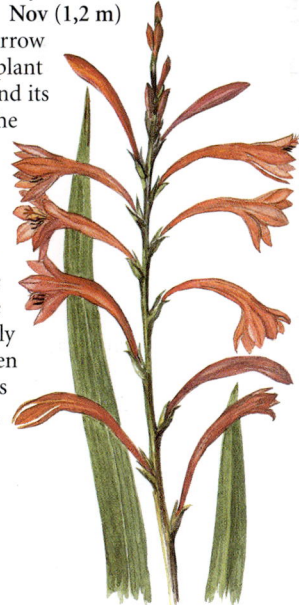

◄ Candelabra Flower ▼
Brunsvigia orientalis
Feb - Apr (50 - 80 cm)
A single stalk grows up from the sandy soil, ending in a large cluster (about 40 cm across) of crimson flowers. The flower-head becomes papery when it dries, and it breaks off and rolls in the wind dispersing seeds. The leaves, which grow from the bulb after the flowers die, lie almost flat on the ground.

Dried flowerhead

FYNBOS

HERBAL AND MEDICINAL

Plants have been harvested for their valuable medicinal and herbal properties from the earliest times. Today, there is growing interest in rediscovering and identifying new health products from fynbos plants. The plants, however, need to be harvested wisely, to prevent over-exploitation and loss of biodiversity.

▲ Carpet Geranium ►
Geranium incanum
Sep - Jan (up to 30 cm)
Low-growing, this plant has fine leaves and grows in large patches on road verges, like a carpet. The flowers vary from pale-pink to purple. An infusion made from this plant is used to treat venereal diseases, menstruation problems and bladder infections.

Rose-scented Pelargonium ►
Pelargonium capitatum
Sep - Jan (30 - 90 cm)
This low bush has straggly branches and velvety, crinkly leaves with small pink to purple flowers. Apart from the flowers, the plant is covered with long, soft, white hairs. If crushed it has a pleasant smell, and is one of the species cultivated for geranium oil. Rubbed onto skin, the leaves soothe scratches and calouses.

Ivy-leafed Pelargonium ►
Pelargonium peltatum
Oct - Jan (climber)
Climbing over shrubs and trees, the leaves of this creeper resemble an ivy leaf and are fleshy and glossy. The sour-tasting leaves are used to soothe sore throats, and when pounded, can be made into a useful antiseptic for skin abrasions and minor burns. The flowers grow at the end of short stalks, and are pink to mauve with darker markings on the upper two petals.

◄ Sorrel
Oxalis purpurea **Apr - Sep (3 cm)**
The flowers of the Sorrel are deep purplish-red with yellow centres. The leaves are broad, heart-shaped and arranged in threes, like clovers. Early in the 17th Century, it was discovered that eating Sorrel leaves was very beneficial to sailors suffering from scurvy.

▼ Honeybee ►
Apis mellifera **(15 mm)**
These bees feed on nectar and pollen which they carry in pollen sacs on their hind legs. They live in a social colony with a single queen bee. They make 'honeycomb' nests.

◄ Minaret Flower (Wildedagga) ▼
Leonotis leonurus **Mar - Jul (2 m)**
Although commonly called 'wild dagga', because of its strong-smelling leaves, it has no narcotic properties. The plant is nevertheless traditionally used for the treatment of skin disorders and snake bite, and for headaches and coughs. This tall shrub has 'box-like' stems and orange-red, velvety flowers. The narrow leaves are paired and rough, and it grows on dune-scrub and open mountain slopes.

Dried flower-heads

◀ **Dune Salvia (Wild Sage)**
Salvia aurea
May - Jan (1 m)
Dune Salvia can be very bushy, and has soft, silvery-grey, strong-smelling leaves. The flowers are yellowish-brown. The greenish-purple seed-pockets stay on the plant long after the flowers have died. The leaves may be used in cooking as a substitute for the herb sage.

September-bush Polygala ▼
Polygala myrtifolia
May - Dec (2,5 m)
This wide bush grows in a variety of habitats. It has narrow, leathery, shiny, green leaves with large, mauve to purple-pink flowers resembling butterflies. Muslims used to boil the bark, and use the water to wash their dead. The leaves were used as a poultice to relieve the pain of gout.

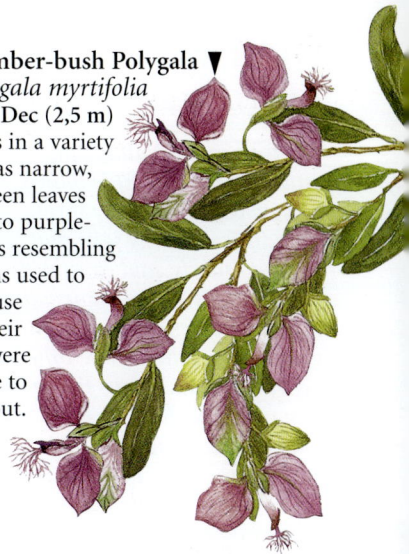

White Bristle-bush ▶ (Blombos)
Metalasia muricata
Jan - Dec (2 m)
White Bristle-bush is a widespread, variable shrub that grows from sea level to high altitudes. It is traditionally used to make a refreshing cup of tea.

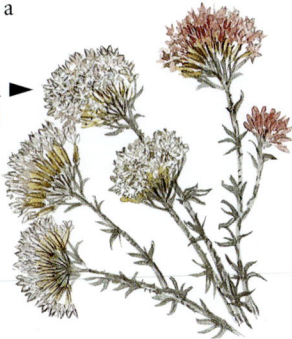

Carpenter Bee ▶
Family Xylocopinae
(10 - 35 mm)
Carpenter bees build nests in dry wood, including dead trees, stems of a dead Aloe, or dry timber in buildings.

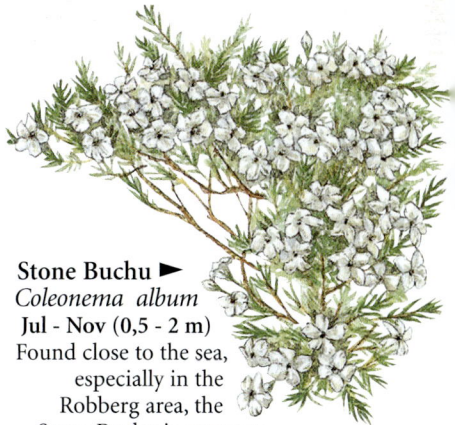

◀ **Mountain Buchu**
Agathosma ciliaris **Jun - Nov (up to 40 cm)**
Very abundant from Still Bay to Mossel Bay, the Mountain Buchu is found on granite or sandstone ridges. As with all buchus it releases a strong-smelling oil, particularly when the leaves are crushed, and it makes a good addition to potpourris. Several species of this family form the basis of a small buchu-oil industry.

▼ **Buchu**
Agathosma capensis **Aug - Apr (0,5 - 1,5 m)**
Buchus are woody members of the citrus family, growing on sunny mountain slopes and in coastal scrub. The round clusters of small flowers vary in colour from white, pink, mauve to bluish-purple. The lower stems are woody, whilst the upper parts are surrounded by tiny, very strong-smelling leaves. When crushed they release oils that are used to flavour ice-cream, jam and cooldrinks, and are also added to perfumes. Extracts of the plant are used to treat indigestion and hangovers.

Stone Buchu ▶
Coleonema album
Jul - Nov (0,5 - 2 m)
Found close to the sea, especially in the Robberg area, the Stone Buchu is common among rocks and on ledges. This evergreen, woody shrub is a useful garden plant as it forms an attractive backdrop, even without the flowers. The tiny oil-glands on the surface of leaves, fruits and petals, release an aromatic oil used for making perfumes and diuretic medicines.

DUNE AND ESTUARIES

Life isn't easy for dune and estuarine plants. Dune plants have to cope with salty spray from the sea, sandy soils that dry out quickly, and constantly shifting sand. Some plants adapt by having thick, fleshy, tough leaves which store water, while others have no leaves at all. Plants living around estuaries have high levels of salt in the mud and sand. Reeds and sedges, which often grow in dense bands, are well suited to this.

TREES AND BUSHES

Woody vegetation lines the banks of estuaries providing perches for water birds, such as cormorants and kingfishers. Amongst the dunes, bush clumps and thickets provide shelter to shy antelope, such as duiker and grysbok. Invasive Australian Acacias are rapidly replacing the native dune vegetation, and drastically changing the ecology of the dunes.

Many plants grow close to the ground, stabilising the sand and allowing others to gain a hold. Dunes are fragile eco-systems and very sensitive to trampling.

◀ **White Milkwood** ▼
Sideroxylon inerme
Jan - Jul (10 m) 579
Evergreen
These small trees, often with twisted barks, form dense thickets in coastal areas and dry forests. The leaves are leathery, dark-green above and paler below; the flowers are green-white; the bark and purple-black berries contain a milky fluid. The 'Post Office Tree' in Mossel Bay is a national monument (see page 109), and all White Milkwoods are protected by law.

◀ **Crossberry Raisin** ▼
Grewia occidentalis
Aug - Mar (6 m) 463
Evergreen
This shrub has pale-grey, smooth bark, light-green leaves and star-shaped, pink-mauve flowers. It grows in coastal forest and shrub. It has four-lobed, square, yellow-orange fruit which is brownish-red when ripe. The bark, soaked in hot water, is said to heal wounds.

▼ **Narrow-leaved Camphor-bush (Wild Camphor Bush)**
Tarchonanthus camphoratus
Mar - May (9 m) 733
Evergreen
A small tree with leathery leaves that are grey-green above and cream-coloured below. When crushed they smell of camphor. Both the cream-white flowers and the seeds are covered with white hairs. It grows in dune-scrub and at the edge of forests.

Dune Guarri (Sea Guarri) ▼
Euclea racemosa
Dec - Mar (6 m) 599 Evergreen
The bark of this small tree is smooth and grey, and its leaves are thick and leathery, paler green below than above. It has small cream-white flowers and black berries, and grows in coastal forest and dune-scrub.

◄ Krantz Aloe
Aloe arborescens
Apr - Jul
(2 - 3 m)
Each branch bears a rosette of curved prickly leaves from which 4 - 5 flowering stems grow. Clusters of orange or scarlet flowers form a cone shape at the top of each stem. It grows in rocky mountain passes and on coastal cliffs and dunes.

Bushtick-berry ►
(Bietou)
Chrysanthemoides monilifera
May - Sep
(2 m) 736.1
Evergreen
This shrub has leathery, grey-green, glossy leaves which are covered with white, cobweb-like hairs when young. Its flowers are bright-yellow and daisy-like. Birds love to eat the black-purple berries.

Waxy Currant-rhus ▼
(Glossy Currant Bush)
Rhus lucida Aug - Oct
(3 - 4 m) 388.1 Evergreen
This small tree has shiny, leathery leaves, small, cream-white flowers, and small, shiny brown berries. The hard, tough wood is good for fence posts.

Horsefly ►
Family
Tabanidae
(10 - 25 mm)
Horseflies feed on nectar and pollen. The females have piercing mouth parts and also suck blood. The larvae feed on small insects, tadpoles or worms.

▼ Blue-fruit Currant-rhus
(Dune Crow-berry) *Rhus crenata*
Feb - Mar (2 m) 380.1 Evergreen
With a strong but pleasant scent, the thin, leathery leaves are dark grey-green above and yellow-green below. It has small, white-cream flowers in the autumn and black berries in the winter.

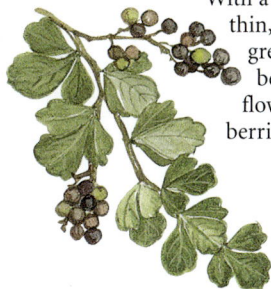

Dune Olive ►
(Coast Olive)
Olea exasperata
Nov - Feb
(1 - 7 m) 619
Evergreen
This shrub has leathery, paired leaves, and clusters of white flowers grow at the tips of leafless twigs. Its oval fruit is purple-black. In the past the root was used as an antidote for snake-bites.

◄ Candleberry (Waxberry)
Myrica cordifolia
Jun - Oct (up to 2 m) Evergreen
The Candleberry has small bluish berries, covered with white waxy scales which the early Cape settlers used for making candles and soap. The plant has long underground stems from which many new plants grow.

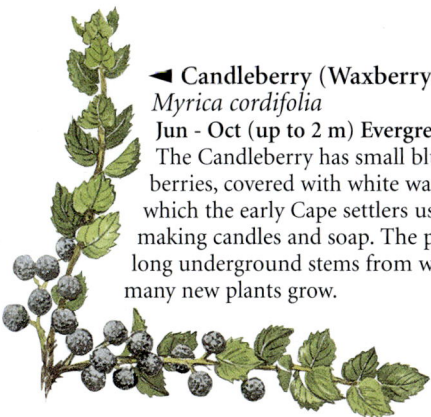

DUNE AND ESTUARIES

LOW LYING PLANTS

The low-lying plants are those that creep over the surface of the sand-dunes and never grow very high. They help to stabilise the dunes, and to prevent excessive wind erosion and movement of sand. These plants have shallow root-systems, and are able to use any surface water, before it drains away into the sand.

◄ **Sea Lavender** ►
Limonium scabrum
Jul - Jan (30 cm)
This plant has a rosette of blue-green leaves at its base, and branched stems with many pale-mauve, papery flowers.

▼ **Oranjegousblom**
Gazania krebsiana **Aug - Nov (20 cm)**
Low-growing, without a proper stem and with variable-shaped leaves, this plant has yellow-orange flowers which may be up to 5 cm wide. It grows in dry grassland and along the edge of roads.

◄ **Seeplakkie** ▲
Scaevola plumieri
Nov - Apr (45 cm)
This is a creeping plant with woody stems and white flowers that grow in clusters from the base of the large, leathery leaves. It grows on sandy shores just above the high-tide level and stabilises shifting sand-dunes.

Sea Pumpkin ▼
Arctotheca populifolia
Sep - May (30 cm)
The thick, rounded leaves are covered with silvery hairs, and its yellow flowers have 'petals' which are indented at the tip. It grows at river mouths and on coastal sand dunes.

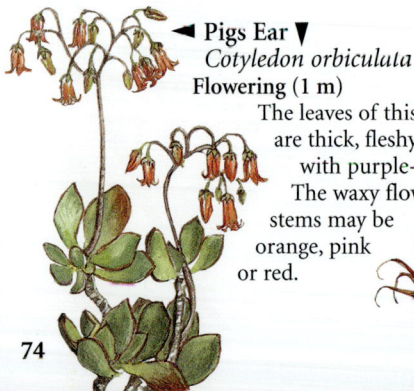

◄ **Sour Fig** ►
Carpobrotus deliciosus
Aug - Oct (creeper)
The long branches, with thick, fleshy leaves trail along the ground with roots anchoring them to the sand at various points. The flowers are large, satiny-purple with yellow centres. The ripe fruit is sweet and juicy.

◄ **Pigs Ear** ▼
Cotyledon orbiculata
Flowering (1 m)
The leaves of this poisonous plant are thick, fleshy and grey-green with purple-red tinged edges. The waxy flowers on long stems may be orange, pink or red.

Dried flower-heads

▲ **Soutbossie**
Chenolea diffusa **Jan - Feb (10 cm)**
Growing low on the ground, it is a straggling, red-stemmed plant with silver-grey leaves, which become orange or red. It has very tiny, yellow flowers. It grows on rocks, banks and in sand at the edge of coastal rivers and lagoons.

▲ Wild Cineraria

Senecio elegans **Aug - Mar (60 cm)**
This plant has purple flowers with yellow centres.
Its leaves are finely notched, and are thinner and
juicier on plants growing near the sea.

Christmas Berry ►

Chironia baccifera
Sep - Mar (45 cm)
This little shrub, with
small, narrow leaves, forms
a round bush with brilliant
pink flowers, followed by
bright orange-red berries. It
grows on coastal sand dunes
and on sunny mountain slopes.

▲ Coastal Buffalo Grass

Strenotaphrum secundatum **(up to 20 cm)**
Prefering sandy soils near the sea or fresh water
sources, it is commonly used for golf-course lawns.

Glasswort Samphire ▼

Sarcocornia perennis
(30 mm)
A sprawling perennial
succulent, it forms mats on
estuarine mudflats, and is
submerged at high tide.

▼Bulrush ►

Typha latifolia capensis
Dec - Mar/Jul - Sep (2 m)
Amongst the long, narrow
leaves of this plant are
tall stems with
spikes of flowers.
The yellow, male
flowers, on the upper
part of the spike, fall off after
pollination leaving the brown
'bulrush' of female flowers. It
grows in marshy ground.

▼ Dune Slack Rush ►

Juncus kraussii
**Dec - Jan
(1 - 1,5 m)**
This is one of several sedge
species which borders
estuaries in the Garden
Route area.

◄ Reeds ►

Phragmites australis
**Dec - Jun
(0,6 - 4 m)**
The flowering stems
of this reed are
feathery, and it grows
in wet places such as
river beds.

◄ Dune Ehrharta ►

Ehrharta villosa
Oct - Apr (90 cm)
This grass grows in
shady moist places, often
at forest edges.

LAND MAMMALS

The diversity and abundance of mammal species increases from the coastline inland. This is because of the changes in vegetation and availability of suitable habitats. Each animal favours specific types of habitat. Some are able to live across a wide range of habitats, like the bushpig, while others can only live in specific habitat types, such as the Cape Clawless Otter. Many of the mammals share habitats, but each has its own lifestyle. Some are arboreal (moving above the ground), like the Vervet Monkey (but they also spend time foraging on the ground); others are fossorial (living in burrows), like the Cape Dune Molerat; while others are entirely terrestrial (living on the ground), like the antelope.

The numbers of mammal species in the southern Cape has declined or disappeared because of hunting, the development of towns and farms, and other human activities. Today, only two elephants, an old female and a young bull, roam the Knysna Forest (page 109).

> *Mammals are measured in height*
> *H - ground to shoulder, or in length*
> *L - tip of nose to tip of tail.*

The solitary Cape Clawless Otter enjoying a fishy snack

MAMMALS

Mammals occupy different feeding niches. They may be carnivores (meat-eaters), herbivores (plant-eaters), insectivores (insect-eaters), frugivores (fruit-eaters) or omnivores (a mix of different diets). The herbivores include browsers, (animals that eat leaves, stems and seeds) and grazers (those that prefer grasses), and therefore make use of different parts of the vegetation. The Cape Grysbok and Common and Blue Duiker are nocturnal (active during the night), but have been illustrated here with the other antelope.

It is illegal to hunt animals without a permit. Animal numbers are already threatened by loss of habitat, therefore limits are set on when and where hunting can take place. Please respect our wildlife.

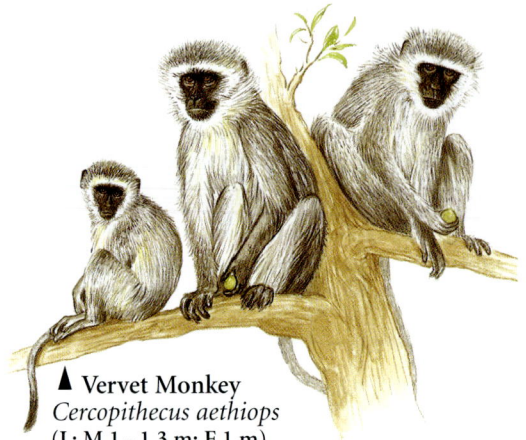

▲ Vervet Monkey
Cercopithecus aethiops
(L: M 1 - 1,3 m; F 1 m)
Vervet Monkeys are found in riverine woodlands, in troops of up to twenty. They sleep in tall trees and forage during the day, on the ground and in trees, searching for wild fruit, birds, eggs and insects.

◄ Chacma Baboon
Papio ursinus
(L: M 1,2 - 1,6 m; F 1 - 1,2 m)
Baboons prefer mountains, hills and forests with tall trees or rocky cliffs for shelter. They live in troops of 20 - 100 individuals, and forage during the day for a wide range of food, including fruit, leaves, flowers, insects, mice, birds and even young antelope.

▼ Small and Large Grey Mongoose
Galerella pulverulenta / Herpestes ichneumon
(L: 55 - 69 cm / 1 m)
The Small Grey Mongoose depicted here, lives in a variety of habitats, from forest to open scrub, eating insects, mice and birds. Its legs are darker than the rest of its body. The Large Grey Mongoose has a black tail-tip, long hair around the back legs, and eats small animals, even Puff Adders.

Dassie ►▼
(Rock Hyrax)
Procavia capensis
(L: 45 - 60 cm)
Dassies live in groups and like to sunbathe on rocky outcrops with one member of the group standing guard for predators, such as Black Eagles. They also climb trees. Dassies eat grass, leaves, fruit and bark. Their closest relative is the elephant (page 109)!

▼ Cape Dune Molerat
Bathyergus suillus (L: M 33 cm; F 30 cm)
The body of these molerats is light-brown. They live underground in sandy soil where they feed on roots and bulbs.

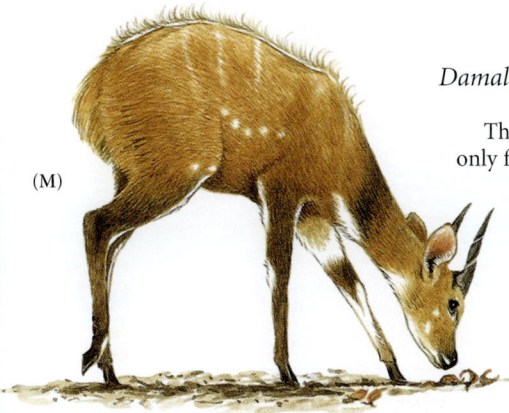

(M)

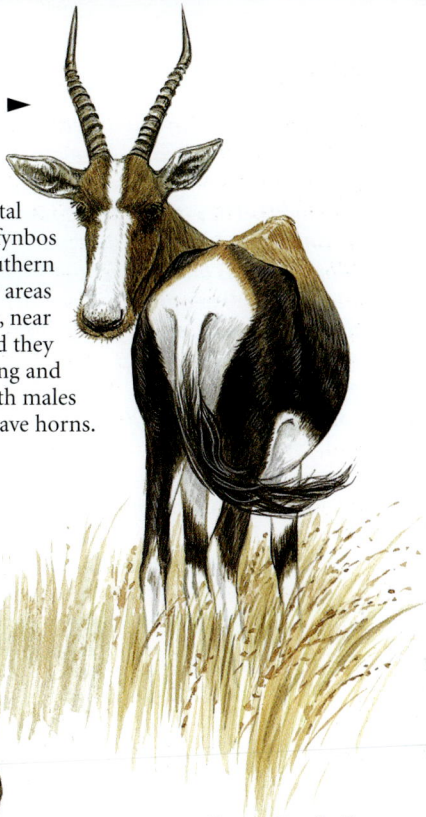

Bontebok ►
Damaliscus dorcas dorcas
(H: 90 cm)
These rare antelope are
only found in a small coastal
plain region with fynbos
vegetation in the southern
Cape. They prefer areas
with short grass, near
water sources, and they
graze in the morning and
late afternoon. Both males
and females have horns.

▲ **Southern Cape Bushbuck**
Tragelaphus scriptus (H: M 80 cm; F 70 cm)
These timid, medium-sized antelope live near water, from
coastal dune bush to mountain forests. They are usually
seen alone and feed mostly at night, browsing on a variety
of plants. Only males have horns.

Blue Duiker ►
Philantomba monticola
(H: M 30 cm; F 32 cm)
The Blue Duiker is the smallest southern
African antelope. The upperparts vary from
slate-grey to dark-brown with a
grey-blue sheen, and the
underparts are white. Living in
dense forests and bush near water
sources, they eat mainly fallen leaves,
fruit and flowers, and often follow troops of
monkeys, eating the food that is dropped from
the trees. Both males and females have horns.

Dung Beetle ▼
Subfamily Scarabaeinae
Insect (5 - 50 mm)
Dung Beetles vary in colour.
They feed on the dung
of plant-eating mammals.
Most species roll dung
into balls and bury
them for later use.
They are strong
flyers although
rather clumsy.

(M)

◄ Common Duiker
Sylvicapra grimmia
(H: M 50 cm; F 70 cm)
Common Duikers prefer scrub and
bush-covered country. They are found
in undergrowth and thickets
browsing on leaves, fruit, flowers
and seeds. They also dig for
tubers and roots. Only the
males have horns.

▲ **Rhinoceros
Beetle**
Oryctes boas
Insect (30 mm)
The male beetles
have a horn
which they use in
fights with other
males. The larvae,
large white grubs,
are often found in
rotting vegetation
or animal dung.

Cape Grysbok ►
Raphicerus melanotis (H: 54 cm)
Active mainly at night, these animals are found
on their own or in pairs. They live in fairly
thick scrub-bush in fynbos. Grysbok are
selective feeders, foraging for palatable
grasses, herbs, leaves, fruit and pods.
Only the males have horns.

(M)

79

Mainly Nocturnal

Mammals are active at different times. Those illustrated here are mainly nocturnal (active during the night). They often fill the same or similar niches as the diurnal (day) animals but use them at night. They are well adapted to a nocturnal lifestyle. Some have very large eyes to capture as much light as possible, while others compensate with excellent hearing and/or smell.

These mammals are often common, but infrequently seen because of their nocturnal habits. A spotlight is the best way of sighting these creatures as their shining eyes can easily be spotted in the dark.

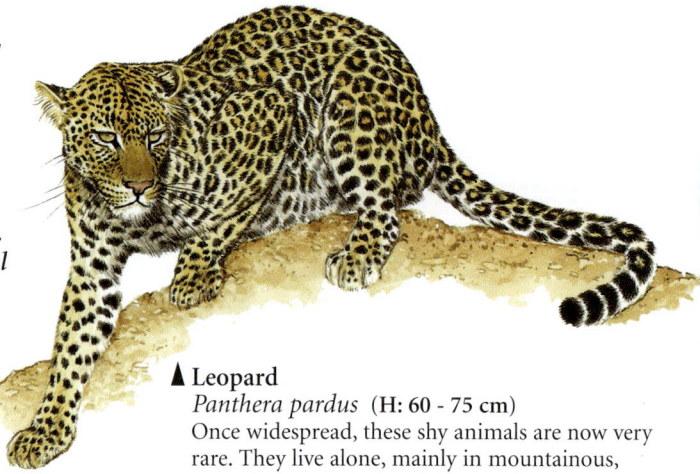

▲ Leopard
Panthera pardus (H: 60 - 75 cm)
Once widespread, these shy animals are now very rare. They live alone, mainly in mountainous, rugged areas. Active at night, they hunt mice, dassies, bushpigs and medium-sized antelope. They often hide their prey from other predators by hauling it up trees or dragging it under bushes.

▲ Cape Serotine Bat
Eptesicus capensis (L: 8,5 cm)
These bats are high fliers and they eat insects. They gather in small numbers in rock crevices, roofs or trees.

Cape Hare ►
Lepus capensis (L: 45 - 60 cm)
Cape Hares prefer dry, open grassland areas. They eat plants and get moisture from their food and the dew. Although active at night, they may also be seen in the early morning or late afternoon, usually on their own.

Vlei Rat ►
Otomys irroratus (L: 24 cm)
Vlei Rats are seen during the day in marshy areas or damp grasslands. They eat shoots and stems of grass, sedges, reeds and other plants. Their saucer-shaped nests are built on dry, raised ground or in clumps of grass.

▲ Egyptian Fruit Bat
Rousettus aegyptiacus
(L: 15 cm)
Living in forests and riverine woodlands, these bats often shelter in caves or old mine-shafts. They eat ripe fruit.

Striped Mouse ►
Rhabdomys pumilio (L: 18 - 21 cm)
Striped Mice live in grassy areas. They eat insects, seeds and other plant material, including the fleshy parts of Protea flowers which they help to pollinate. They are the most common mice found in the fynbos region, and are an important food source for many predators. They dig long, chambered burrows or build round nests in clumps of grass.

◄ **Caracal**
Felis caracal
(H: 40 - 45 cm)
Caracals occur
throughout the
southern Cape, from
fynbos to forest. They
are nocturnal, solitary and
secretive, hunting mainly birds and
small- to medium-sized mammals.
Their fur colour varies according to region.

▲ **Small- and Large-spotted Genet**
Genetta genetta / Genetta tigrina
(L: 85 - 100 cm)
Genets usually hunt at night and feed on
insects, mice, frogs and birds. The
Small-spotted Genet has white facial
markings and a white tail-tip. The
Large-spotted Genet has a black tail-tip.

Cape Clawless Otter ►
Aonyx capensis (L: 1 - 1,3 m)
These solitary otters swim in both
fresh and sea water. They dive in
search of frogs, crabs, fish,
octopus and also eat insects,
birds and reptiles.

Cape Porcupine ▼
Hystrix africaeaustralis (L: 84 - 86 cm)
They are the largest southern African rodents.
Living in a variety of habitats, usually alone,
they are mainly active at night, often
spending the day in caves or burrows. They
dig for tubers, bulbs and roots but also eat
fruit and gnaw bark off trees.

▲ **Water Mongoose**
Atilax paludinosus (L: 80 - 100 cm)
Living near shallow water, these
mongooses dig in the mud to find crabs
and mussels, which they throw onto the
rocks to break their shells. They also eat
frogs, rodents, birds, fish and insects.

◄ **Bushpig**
Potamochoerus larvatus
(H: M 76 cm; F 65 cm)
Active at night, these animals live in groups of 7 - 12,
in forests, bush or reed-beds, near water. They dig for
plant bulbs and tubers with their snouts, and also eat
earthworms, insects, fruit and carrion.

81

REPTILES AND AMPHIBIANS

Unlike mammals (endotherms), reptiles and amphibians (ectotherms) control their body temperature by external means, that is from the sun. Lizards are often seen basking in the sun in the morning to warm up their bodies. The advantage is that they do not have to eat as much food as warm-blooded animals, but must hibernate during winter. Reptiles differ from frogs in that they have dry, scaly skin and do not need moisture to survive. Some reptiles, however, are well adapted to an aquatic lifestyle (pages 84 - 85).

Amphibians are most plentiful in good rainy years, when they emerge from hibernation to breed. The rainfall along the Garden Route, however, occurs throughout most of the year, and therefore frogs may be found breeding here at any time.

Many reptile and amphibian populations have suffered as a result of human activities. Amphibians are threatened by the loss of wetland areas, while turtle numbers are rapidly declining because they are eaten, and their breeding sites are disturbed.

Reptiles and amphibians are measured in length from tip of nose to tip of tail.

The Angulate Tortoise ambling slowly in search of food.

WATERBASED

The amphibians (frogs and toads) and some reptiles are adapted to a water-based environment. Amphibians, although not always dependent on standing bodies of water, need moist (fresh water) habitats to live and breed. Their slimy, porous skin does not prevent water loss, and they will dry out from lack of moisture. The two turtle species and the sea snake are marine reptiles, well adapted to sea life, with salt secreting glands to rid the body of excess salt.

Toads differ from frogs in having dry, rough skin, which excretes a white mucus when threatened. The statement that "toads give you warts" is an old wives' tale.

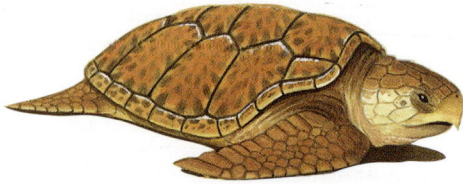

▲ **Common Brown Water Snake**
Lycodonomorphus rufulus (60 - 87 cm)
These harmless snakes are olive to brown, with light pink-yellow bellies and lips, living near rivers and streams. At night, they hunt frogs, tadpoles and fish, squeezing the prey before swallowing it.

◄ **Yellow-bellied Sea Snake**
Pelamis platurus (0,6 - 1 m)
Living in tropical seas, these poisonous snakes feed on small fish. Their flat, bar-like tails are good for swimming.

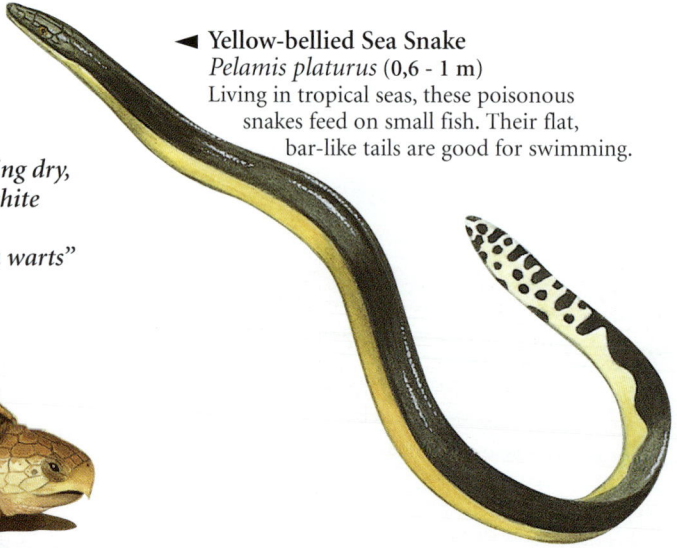

Loggerhead Turtle ▲
Caretta caretta (1,5 m)
Loggerhead Turtles drift in the deep sea when young, feeding on floating animals. When older, they move closer to shore and feed on crabs, sea urchins and molluscs.

Cape Sand Frog ►
Tomopterna delalandei (up to 5 cm)
Although restricted to fresh water for breeding, the Cape Sand Frog also forages on sandy beaches for small invertebrates. It occurs in open sand and grassland habitats and has a prominent 'spade' on its heel for digging backwards into the sandy soil when preparing to hibernate.

Leatherback Turtle ▼
Dermochelys coriacea
(2,5 - 3 m)
These rare turtles are the heaviest living reptiles. They have clawless flippers for swimming, and eat jellyfish and bluebottles. They live out at sea and usually return to the same beaches to lay their eggs.

◄ Clicking Stream Frog ►
Strongylopus grayii
(4,5 - 6 cm)
The repeated, short, sharp calls of these frogs can be heard throughout the year even in winter. Eggs are laid in a capsule of stiff jelly.

Arum Lily Frog ►
Hyperolius horstockii
(3,5 cm)
These frogs are found in reeds, often far from water, and in the flowers of Arum Lilies where they become whitish in colour. They have suckers on all their toes and fingers.

◄ Banded Stream Frog
Strongylopus bonaspei
(4 cm)
The Banded Stream Frog prefers marshy ground and seepage areas of mountain streams. It has brown-orange stripes on its back, a pointed snout and very long toes. It is an exceptionally good jumper, and can cover two metres in a single leap. The 'plops' you hear as you stroll along a river bank are most likely made by these frogs.

▼ Cape River Frog
Rana fuscigula (7,5 cm; up to 12 cm)
A large, common frog, the Cape River Frog is usually detected when it 'plops' into nearby water for safety. Males, calling from deep water support themselves on floating vegetation in permanent ponds, streams and rivers. They have webbed hind toes because they are more aquatic than terrestrial.

◄ Common Caco
Cacosternum boettgeri (2,3 cm)
The Common Caco favours any marshy wetlands and swamp grasslands where the water is shallow. It calls from the base of vegetation in high-pitched clicks, day and night. Cacos hide for most of the year but are very abundant after good rains.

◄ ▼ Raucous Toad
Bufo rangeri
(up to 10 cm)
As its name implies, the Raucous Toad has a very loud, rasping 'kwaak, kwaak'. It calls from exposed areas near the water or from rocks in shallow water. It is found in open and bush areas, and is also common in gardens. Different colour variations are found.

Calling

Common Platanna ▼
Xenopus laevis (7 cm)
They are aquatic frogs that breed and feed underwater, eating insects and snails, as well as small animals and nestlings that fall into the water. Breeding is from early spring to late summer. The eggs are attached to submerged grass, stones and sticks.

Common Platanna tadpoles

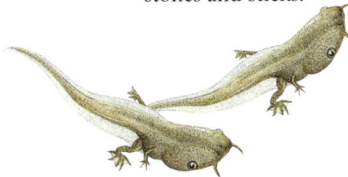

LANDBASED

Reptiles can live away from water because of their dry, horny skin, and have successfully inhabited most environments. Most of these reptiles are generalists, occurring in a wide range of habitat types. They do, however, require shelter, such as rocks or scrub, for hibernating and resting, and will therefore seldom be found along the beaches. The Southern Rock Agama, however, may be found foraging amongst washed-up debris along the high watermark.

The vast majority of our snakes, and all our lizards, are not poisonous, and are therefore totally harmless. Like most animals, the few dangerous snakes only harm when threatened.

Angulate Tortoise ▶
Chersina angulata
(16 - 26 cm)
Angulate Tortoises feed mostly on grasses and other plants, and at shallow pools, drinking water through their noses.

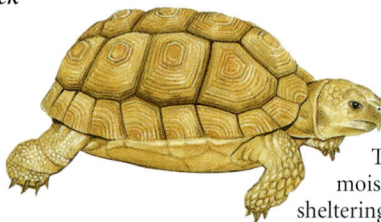

◀ Common Padloper
Homopus areolatus
(12 cm)
They are found in the moister coastal regions, often sheltering under rocks or in disused animal burrows. The female lays 2 - 3 eggs in a small nest hole in shady soil. They can live up to 30 years in captivity.

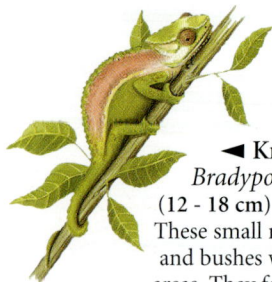

◀ Knysna Dwarf Chameleon
Bradypodion damaranum
(12 - 18 cm)
These small reptiles blend into the trees and bushes where they live in wet coastal areas. They feed on insects at night.

◀ Marble Leaf-toed Gecko ▼
Phyllodactylus porphyreus (8 - 10 cm)
Active at night, these geckos often feed on insects around outside lights. When provoked, geckos may click, chirp and squeal.

Cape Skink ▶
Mabuya capensis
(20 - 27 cm)
Cape Skinks feed mainly on insects such as grasshoppers and beetles. They live in tunnels which they dig in loose soil.

(M)

Plain Rain Frog ▼
Breviceps fuscus (5 cm)
These frogs are found in coastal mountains from Knysna to Swellendam. They live in shallow tunnels up to 15 cm deep, or on the forest floor in moist, shady spots. Their loud chirruping call, which is repeated at short intervals, sounds like a police whistle.

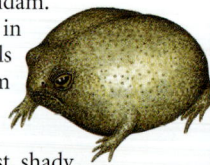

◀ Southern Rock Agama ▶
Agama atra
(20 - 32 cm)
Often seen basking on rocky outcrops, these lizards eat ants and termites. The male lizards bob their heads to warn off intruders, or possibly to attract females.

(F)

Cape Cobra
Naja nivea
(1,2 - 1,7 m)
When disturbed, these very poisonous snakes raise their bodies and spread a 'hood' just below the head. Colour varies from yellow to reddish-brown, even black. In the day they hunt rats, mice, lizards, frogs and other snakes.

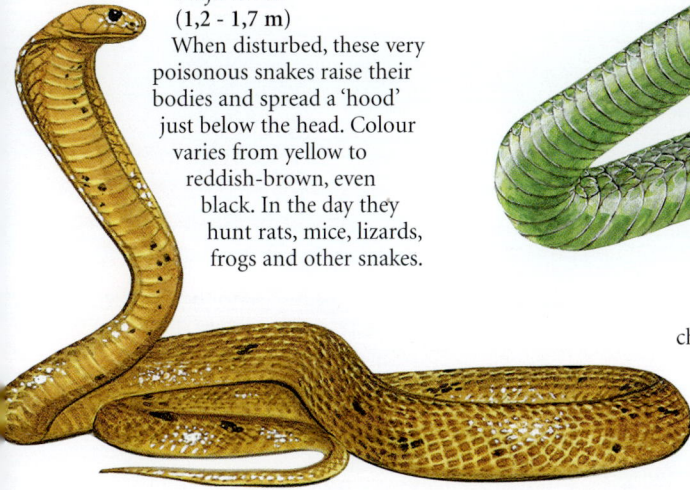

Boomslang ▲
Dispholidus typus
(1,2 - 2 m)
Also called 'tree-snakes', these very poisonous reptiles live mainly in trees. During the day they hunt chameleons, lizards and young birds.

Puff Adder ►
Bitis arietans (0,7 - 2 m)
Puff Adders are very poisonous, slow-moving snakes. They often bask in the sun in grass or bush, or across footpaths. They eat mainly rats and mice.

Olive House Snake ▼
Lamprophis inornatus (0,6 - 1,3 m)
Found mostly in damp places, these harmless snakes eat rats, mice, frogs and sometimes other snakes.

Common Slug-eater
Duberria lutrix (30 - 43 cm)
Living in damp places, these harmless snakes eat snails and slugs. When alarmed they roll up into a spiral.

▲ Common or Rhombic Egg-eater
Dasypeltis scabra (0,5 - 11,6 m)
When threatened, these harmless snakes coil up and rub their scales against one another to make a loud hissing noise. They only eat birds' eggs, which they swallow whole.

BIRD LIFE

There is a rich diversity of bird species occurring along the Garden Route because of the wide range of habitats. Birds require specific habitat conditions that will provide them with the rich food supply needed for survival, and also the sheltered sites for nesting and breeding. Some birds occur only in one type of habitat, like some of the Cape fynbos species; others range across a wide variety of habitats, like the Hadeda Ibis. Endemic birds (usually originating in the area) are very vulnerable to habitat loss, as their feeding and breeding needs are so specific.

Bird watching is a great hobby for people of all ages. Knowing distribution and habitat preferences is the first step in identification. The next step is recognising the different bill shapes and body proportions of the different bird groups. To save hours of frustrating peering into thick vegetation, try enticing the birds out by 'spishing'. This is a series of short, loud sounds made through one's teeth sounding like a tire deflating in quiet bursts. It is a recognised way of persuading the small and inconspicuous species to reveal themselves.

Birds are numbered with the Roberts number; and their sizes are given from beak-tip to tail-tip.

This solitary Hamerkop waits patiently for a frog meal by a slow-moving river.

WATERBIRDS

Water birds are associated with a wide range of aquatic habitats. These range from salt to fresh water, and from small, temporary pools to large, permanent water bodies. The birds each have a specific niche within this environment. To forage and breed, birds use the banks of water bodies, the water surface itself, deep water and the vegetation on, or surrounding, the water.

SEA AND ROCKY CLIFF BIRDS

Birds that have a close relationship with the seashore have some interesting adaptations that help them cope with their environment. Primarily many are well adapted for swimming. Some of the genuine sea birds, like the Cape Gannet, the Jackass Penguin and the African Black Oystercatcher eat marine animals, and cannot avoid taking in sea water. They have a special adrenal gland that excretes excess salt.

Please don't litter. Littering has a detrimental effect on many water birds, and can cause terrible maiming and often a very slow death. If items such as plastic or string are found lying around water bodies, pick them up and put them in a dustbin.

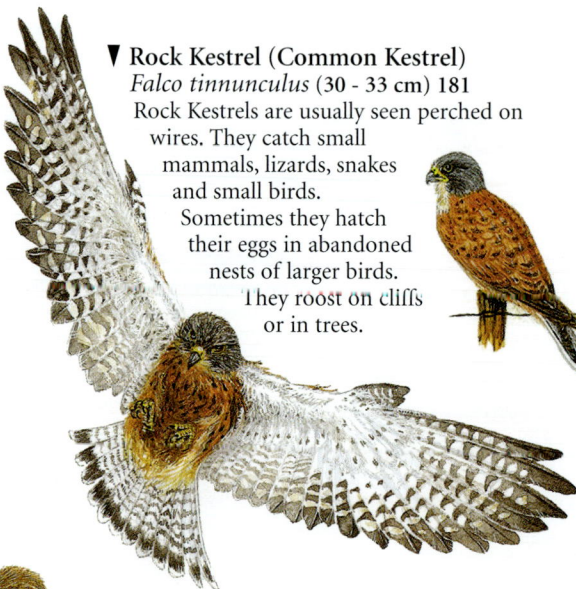

▲ **Kelp Gull**
Larus dominicanus (56 - 60 cm) 312
Kelp Gulls are common and noisy. They have an orange spot on their beaks, and when young chicks peck at it, the adult brings up the food. The gulls eat marine animals, sometimes dropping mussels onto rocks to split them open. They also scavenge.

▼ **Rock Kestrel (Common Kestrel)**
Falco tinnunculus (30 - 33 cm) 181
Rock Kestrels are usually seen perched on wires. They catch small mammals, lizards, snakes and small birds. Sometimes they hatch their eggs in abandoned nests of larger birds. They roost on cliffs or in trees.

House Mouse
(Alien)

◄ **African Black Oystercatcher**
Haematopus moquini (41 cm) 244
Found in pairs or in small groups, they are marine waders. Eating mainly shellfish, they use their flattened beaks to prize them off the rocks and to open their shells. They nest in a shallow 'scrape' on exposed sand, rocks, stones, or next to dried kelp (October to March).

▼ **Cape Cormorant**
Phalacrocorax capensis (61 - 64 cm) 56
These birds are often seen flying one behind the other just behind the breakers. They mainly eat fish, and they nest in shallow hollows lined with twigs and sticks.

▲ Cape Gannet
Morus capensis (84 - 94 cm) 53
These large white birds, with pointed black tails and wing tips, gather at sea in large flocks and follow shoals of fish. They breed only on selected islands. They can be seen plunging into the sea from heights of up to 10 metres, throwing up a fountain of spray.

◄ Swift Tern ►
Sterna bergii (46 - 50 cm) 324
This large tern is found along the coast, where it hunts for fish near the water surface and roosts on beaches.
Its large size and yellow bill are diagnostic. It occurs in gregarious flocks, often with other seabirds such as gulls and other terns.

▼ White-fronted Plover
Charadrius marginatus (18 cm) 246
The White-fronted Plover is usually first spotted running along the shoreline looking for insects. It may also be seen up along the dunes amongst the low-lying vegetation and debris where it nests. It is a very small, squat-looking bird, usually spotted in pairs.

◄ White-breasted Cormorant
Phalacrocorax lucidus (90 cm) 55
These birds often perch on a branch or log to dry their outstretched wings. They eat mainly fish and they nest on ledges. They may also be found inland.

Jackass Penguin ► (African Penguin)
Spheniscus demersus (60 cm) 3
Occuring only in southern Africa, these flightless birds make a sound like braying donkeys. They feed mainly on pilchards. Pollution, over-fishing and egg-collection have caused a serious drop in numbers.

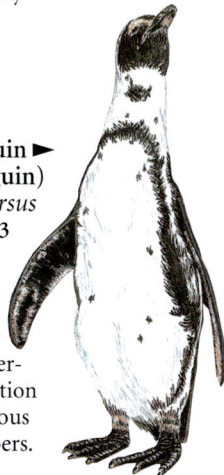

WATERBIRDS

ESTUARIES AND FRESHWATER

The many dams, pans and vleis of the area provide ideal places to see a variety of birds.

Whether they are scavengers or hunters, or eat plants, each has a specialist role to play in the eco-chains. At estuaries the salt waters of the sea meet the nutrient-rich sediments washed down by the rivers. These sediments accumulate as thick mud flats around the river mouths. Many types of shellfish (pages 52 - 53) living in this rich mud, provide food for birds, especially waders.

◀ **African Fish Eagle** ▶
Haliaeetus vocifer
(63 - 73 cm) 148
Fish Eagles have a magnificent call. They hunt fish from a perch, making a shallow dive to catch the fish in their claws. Fish Eagles build their nests in trees.

Flathead Mullet (page 49)

(F)

◀ **Pied Kingfisher**
Ceryle rudis
(25 - 29 cm) 428
These black-and-white birds are usually found in pairs. They are often seen hovering above water looking for fish, but also eat shellfish and insects. They nest in holes in banks.

Giant Kingfisher ▼
Megaceryle maxima
(43 - 46 cm) 429
With speckled black-and-white backs, these are the largest kingfishers. They eat crabs, fish and frogs and nest in holes in streams or river banks.

(M)

Reed Cormorant ▼
Phalacrocorax africanus
(60 cm) 58
The most common of the cormorants, these birds have yellow beaks and long tails. They are often seen with wings stretched out to dry. They eat fish, frogs and aquatic insects.

Malachite Kingfisher ▶
Alcedo cristata (14 cm) 431
This small jewel of a bird is always found near water, usually in pairs. They hunt small fish and tadpoles and nest in holes in a bank.

Egyptian Goose ▼
Alopochen aegyptiacus
(63 - 73 cm) 102
These birds look similar to the South African Shelduck. Their call is a rapid honking made before take-off and sometimes during flight. They eat aquatic plants, grass and seedlings.

Yellow-billed Duck ►
Anas undulata
(51 - 63 cm) 104
The bright yellow bill, with a central black patch, are diagnostic features of Yellow-billed Ducks. They are found in pairs and flocks mostly on both open freshwater but also in estuaries. They feed on plant matter, bottoms-up in deep water, or by grazing on land.

Common Moorhen ►
Gallinula chloropus
(30 - 36 cm) 226
The Common Moorhen is common around many freshwater bodies. It is mostly seen swimming on open water, but also feeds in adjacent wet grasslands. It is very distinctive with its black body, bright red forehead and bill with a yellow tip.

◄ Dragonfly
Suborder
Anisoptera
Insect (wingspan 45 - 140 mm)
These insects can fly up to 80 km per hour! They hunt whilst flying, catching other flying insects and are often seen skimming low over water.

▼ Red-knobbed Coot
Fulica cristata (43 cm) 228
Coots are seen in pairs or large flocks. They feed by dipping under water to pull up aquatic plants. The two red knobs on their heads become larger when the birds breed.

▼ Little Grebe (Dabchick)
Tachybaptus ruficollis (20 cm) 8
When moving fast, Little Grebes look like they are running on the water. They eat a variety of aquatic animals. Their nests are floating platforms made of weeds.

▲ African Darter
Anhinga melanogaster (79 cm) 60
African Darters have slender 'kinked' necks and are also known as 'snakebirds'. They hunt fish underwater, impaling them with their dagger-like beaks. They also catch frogs.

WATERBIRDS

ESTUARIES AND FRESHWATER

Many birds catch food in shallow water or in mud under the water. These waders tend to have long legs which allow them a good view of animal movement beneath the water surface, and a longish bill with which they stab or grab their prey. The Pied Avocet, however, moves its sensitive bill from side-to-side through the water to find potential food. Look out for the amusing sight of waders using their feet to stir up the muddy bottom to disturb possible prey.

▲ **Hamerkop**
Scopus umbretta (**56 cm**) 81
These water birds, with their hammer-shaped heads, are usually found alone or in pairs. Their flattened beaks are well-adapted for catching frogs or carrying large sticks for building their huge nests.

◀ **Little Egret**
Egretta garzetta (**64 cm**) 67
These water birds have black legs with yellow feet and a plume on the back of their heads. They wade in shallow water where they hunt small animals such as tadpoles, fish and crabs.

Grey Heron ▶
Ardea cinerea
(**100 cm**) 62
The large, long-legged Grey Herons have white heads and black eye-stripes which end in a wispy plume at the back of the head. They eat fish, frogs, crabs and insects.

◀ **Blacksmith Lapwing (Plover)**
Vanellus armatus
Wader (**30 cm**) 258
Blacksmith Lapwings are often seen in pairs or small groups. Their call sounds like a hammer on an anvil. They eat insects, worms and small molluscs. Their nests are lined, shallow depressions.

94

Ruff ▼
Philomachus pugnax
(24 - 30 cm) (284)
The Ruff is a summer migrant found
around estuaries and
wetlands. It occurs
singly or in flocks,
and may be seen
wading about in shallow water
probing for invertebrates and
plant matter. The orange legs and
stout bill are diagnostic features
of the adults.

▲ Three-banded Plover
Charadrius tricollaris
Wader (18 cm) 249
This small bird is a
common resident with
double, black breast-
bands that make it
instantly identifiable. It
moves quickly along the
shores and shallows of
inland waters, on its own,
in pairs or small flocks.

◄ Wood Sandpiper
Tringa glareola
(20 cm) 266
The Wood Sandpiper is recognised by
its conspicuous white eyebrow, white
speckles on its back, and green-tinged
legs. It is a common summer visitor, seen
foraging along estuaries and wetlands for
insects and other invertebrates.

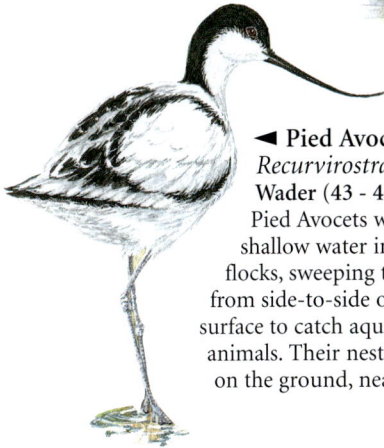

◄ Pied Avocet
Recurvirostra avosetta
Wader (43 - 46 cm) 294
Pied Avocets wade in
shallow water in small
flocks, sweeping their beaks
from side-to-side over the
surface to catch aquatic
animals. Their nests are found
on the ground, near water.

Common ►
Whimbrel
Numenius phaeopus
Wader (43 cm) 290
Common Whimbrels are shy
birds, usually seen alone or in
small groups. They mainly eat crabs, prawns
and shellfish. They have down-curved bills
and two distinct stripes above each eye, one
pale and one dark.

◄ Black-winged Stilt
Himantopus himantopus
Wader (38 cm) 295
Occuring in small flocks, they feed early
or late in the day on insects and worms.
They nest in shallow hollows on
floating vegetation or small islands.

FOREST

These birds use the canopies of the forest to feed and nest, and are therefore more difficult to see. When looking for forest birds, bear in mind that the greatest number are found around the edges or in clearings. This is because these places receive more light, and are where the birds can find warmth, visibility and a richer food source.

Watch carefully and quietly for sudden movement, or flashes of colour which reveal the birds presence.

**Green Wood-Hoopoe ▶
(Red-billed Woodhoopoe)**
Phoeniculus purpureus
(30 - 36 cm) 452
Green Wood-Hoopoes are common, noisy birds, often found in groups. They can be seen examining the trunks and branches of trees looking for food such as nectar, insects, millipedes and lizards. They nest in holes in trees.

(M)

◀ African Paradise-Flycatcher
Terpsiphone viridis
(M 23 - 41 cm
including tail;
F 16 - 18 cm) 710
In breeding season, the male has very long tail feathers. They call and flit about a lot, catching small insects on the wing. They usually nest in the fork of a tree.

**◀ Knysna Turaco
(Knysna Lourie)**
Tauraco corythaix
(45 - 47 cm) 370
The red feathers on these birds' wings are more noticeable in flight. Their call is a trumpet-like *'woop, woop'*, followed by a growling *'korr, korr'*. They eat mainly fruit and build their nests from sticks.

**Sombre Greenbul ▶
(Bulbul)**
*Andropadus
importunus*
(19 - 23 cm) 572
The call of this bird is a distinctive *'weee-wee'* which ends in a drawn-out whistle. They mainly eat fruit and insects and their nests are built at the ends of branches.

◀ Chorister Robin-Chat
Cossypha dichroa (19 - 20 cm) 598
Keeping to the forest canopy, these robins are seldom seen. Their song is a melody of piping trills and whistles, often mimicking other birds. They eat mainly insects and nest in tree holes.

Red-chested Cuckoo ▼
Cuculus solitarius
(28 cm) 377

The Afrikaans name for the
Red-chested Cuckoo is
the Piet-my-vrou, which
is what its call sounds like.
It migrates to southern
Africa to breed in the
summer months when it
is highly vocal
(sometimes even
calling at night). It
parasitises the nests
of the Cape Robin
(see page 111).

▼ Knysna Woodpecker ►
Campethera notata
(20 - 21 cm) 484

On their own, in pairs or in family
groups, they look for ants and beetle
larvae. They nest
in dug-out
tree holes.

(F)

(M)

Black-headed Oriole ►
Oriolus larvatus
(25 cm) 545

This enchanting bird is
mostly heard calling
early morning from the
tops of tall trees in
lively, musical, liquid
notes. The striking
colouration makes it
stand out amongst
the green foliage, and is
therefore easier to spot.
It feeds on insects,
berries and nectar.

Southern Boubou ▼
Laniarius ferrugineus
(22 cm) 736

The shy Southern Boubou is more
often heard than seen because it conceals
itself in the dense undergrowth,
particularly along streams. The male
and female call constantly to each
other to keep in touch. The duet is
variable, with a basic *'boo-boo'*
followed by a whistled
'whee-ooo'.

(M)

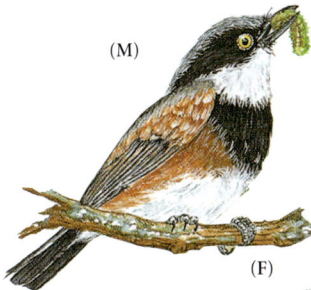

(F)

◄ Cape Batis ▼
Batis capensis (12 - 13 cm) 700

These small, insect-eating birds are usually seen in
pairs. Their nests are small, cup-shaped and
covered with lichen and moss so they
look like part of the tree.

Fynbos

Fynbos provides a unique habitat for birds. It is not surprising therefore that several species occur nowhere else in the world, include the Cape Sugarbird, Orange-breasted Sunbird and Cape Spurfowl. Many fynbos plants are pollinated by birds such as the sunbirds and sugarbirds, which are attracted to the large amounts of sweet nectar produced by the flowers.

When watching birds in fynbos, try to notice which bird pollinates which flower.

◄ **Cape Sugarbird**
Promerops cafer
(M 37 - 44 cm; F 24 - 29 cm) 773
Sugarbirds are larger and less colourful than sunbirds. They mainly eat insects and nectar from Protea flowers. They breed during the winter and build cup-shaped nests in Proteas.

Malachite Sunbird ►
Nectarinia famosa
(M 24 - 26 cm including tail; F 15 cm) 775
Often seen hovering above Aloe or Protea flowers, they eat insects, spiders and nectar. Their oval nests are built over water or in the bank of a dry ravine.

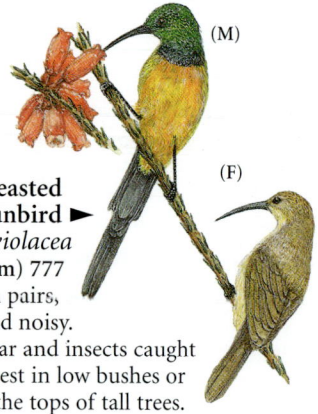

(M)

(M)

(F)

Orange-breasted Sunbird ►
Anthobaphes violacea
(M 17 cm; F 13 cm) 777
Usually occurring in pairs, they are active and noisy. They feed on nectar and insects caught on the wing. They nest in low bushes or in the tops of tall trees.

(M)

Southern Double-collared Sunbird (Lesser Double-collared Sunbird) ▲ ►
Cinnyris chalybea (11 - 13 cm) 783
These birds fly with rapid, swerving movements. They eat insects and nectar. The pear-shaped nest is suspended from the branch of a bush or small tree.

(M)

(F)

Cape Canary ►
Serinus canicollis
(13 - 14 cm) 872
One of the best songsters in the fynbos is the Cape Canary. It is usually seen in flocks next to scrub areas where it forages on the ground or perches on the stems of seeding plants. The grey on the neck and shoulders is diagnostic.

Cape Grassbird ►
Sphenoeacus afer
(19 - 23 cm) 661
When not hunting for
spiders and insects in the
dense vegetation, the
Cape Grassbird is first
seen perching on top of a
grass stem or bush. It is
a fairly large, untidy
looking, streaky-
brown bird with
a rufous crown
and a long
pointed tail.

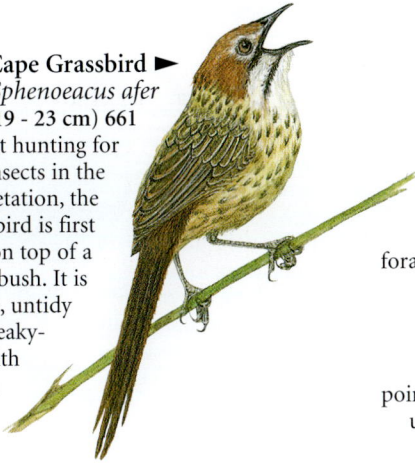

Drakensberg Prinia ►
Prinia hypoxantha
(13 - 15 cm) 686
The Drakensberg Prinia
forages for insects low down
in the grass and bushes
where it is hard to see. If
disturbed, however, it
perches on a vantage
point and flicks it long tail
up over its back and calls
'*kli-kli-kli-
krrrt-krrrt*'.

Ground Woodpecker ▼
Geocolaptes olivaceus
(25 - 30 cm) 480
Unlike other woodpeckers,
they forage on the ground,
mainly for ants. They have
a 'guard' on duty to warn
them of danger. They
nest in holes dug in
river banks.

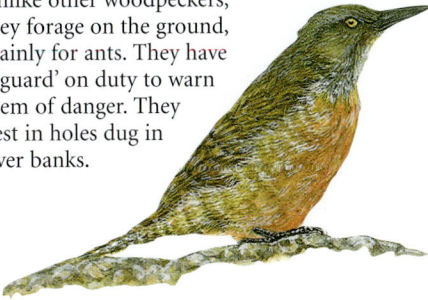

◄ **Cape Bulbul**
Pycnonotus capensis
(19 - 21 cm) 566
An endemic of the Cape
fynbos, the Cape Bulbul
is very vocal and
conspicuous, with
a diagnostic white
wattle around the
eye. It has a fast, bouncy flight, and is
often found in thickets. It feeds on
nectar and fruit.

▼ **Cape Spurfowl** ►
(Francolin)
Pternistes capensis
(40 - 42 cm) 195
These birds are usually
found in thickets, in pairs
or in flocks. They roost in
trees and are very noisy in
the morning and evening.
They eat bulbs, seeds, berries
and insects.

Victorin's Warbler ▼
Bradypterus victorini
(15 - 17 cm) 641
An elusive bird, the Victorin's
Warbler is very difficult to spot.
It spends most its time
foraging between dense
vegetation in the
undergrowth or on the
ground. It is endemic
and confined to the
Cape fynbos.

Sandbathing

99

OTHER COMMON BIRDS

These common birds occur in a wide variety of habitats, from forest to fynbos to coast, and some permanently live in our gardens at home. The Cape White-eye, Common Fiscal and Hadeda Ibis are well adapted to suburbia. The other birds require specific environmental conditions that urban areas cannot often provide, and they therefore do not occur there. The Forest Buzzard depends on forests for survival and will not occur in other habitats. Understanding the specific habitat requirements of any bird will assist with identification.

Nest boxes and food trays will attract many garden birds. However planting trees that are indigenous to the area will establish long-term and healthier relationships with them.

Hadeda Ibis ►
Bostrychia hagedash
(76 cm) 94
Named after their unique call, Hadedas are found in groups, probing the ground for insects, spiders, snails and earthworms. Their nests look like platforms of sticks.

◄ Helmeted Guineafowl
Numida meleagris
(53 - 58 cm) 203
Usually in flocks, these birds wander a lot. They are good runners and scatter and fly up into trees when alarmed. They eat seeds, bulbs, insects and snails, and nest in hollows under bushes.

Black-headed Heron ►
Ardea melanocephala (97 cm) 63
The elegant Black-headed Heron is a solitary feeder, eating frogs, rodents and small birds. The nests are large platforms of sticks.

◄ African Sacred Ibis
Threskiornis aethiopicus
(89 cm) 91
They are usually seen in groups which fly in a 'V' formation. They walk with slow, careful steps as they feed, looking for insects, small mammals, frogs, young birds and birds' eggs.

Cape White-eye ►
Zosterops pallidus
(10 - 13 cm) 796
Usually seen in flocks, these are
sociable birds. They forage widely for
insects, spiders, nectar and fruit. The
cup-shaped nests are suspended in
forks of trees.

Forest Buzzard ►
Buteo trizonatus
(45 cm) 150
Living at forest-edges, they
usually hunt rodents, birds,
lizards and insects. Their
nests are lined platforms of
sticks and are usually found
in forks of trees.

Common Fiscal (Fiscal Shrike) ►
Lanius collaris (21 - 23 cm) 732
Common Fiscals perch on bushes, fences
or telephone wires. They catch insects,
frogs, lizards and bird-chicks which
they impale on thorns and barbed
wire. Their bowl-like nests are
built in the forks of trees.

▼ Cape Wagtail
Motacilla capensis
(19 - 20 cm) 713
These small birds wag their tails
up and down when they
walk. They mainly eat
insects, but also small
shellfish and food
scraps. They will
nest just about
anywhere.

◄ Spotted Eagle-Owl
Bubo africanus
(43 - 47 cm) 401
These common large owls
hunt at night, feeding on rats,
mice, moles and insects. The
male call is a high *'hu- hoo'*
while the female answers with
a lower call. Also found in
rocky and mountain areas.

▼Cape Robin-Chat ►
Cossypha caffra
(16 - 18 cm) 601
Cape Robin-Chats are shy
birds that forage in thick
undergrowth, sometimes
venturing into the open,
nervously jerking their tails.
They eat insects, fruit, small
frogs and lizards, and nest
in thick bush or in crevices.

Fiery-necked Nightjar ▼
Caprimulgus pectoralis
(23 - 25 cm) 405
The call of these common nightjars
sounds like *'Good Lord, deliver us'*.
They hunt insects and spiders at
night and nest on dead leaves and
debris under trees.

Human History

The Outeniqua mountain range snakes grandly along the south-eastern edge of the African continent, and gives the Garden Route its magnificent and ever-changing backdrop.

It was named by an ancient tribe of people who once roamed the area. The word Outeniqua means "man laden with honey", and it is an apt description for this bounteous land which, for close on a million years, has been inhabited by humans.

It is believed that early humans spread outwards from Africa's grasslands and savannahs to colonise the rest of the continent. In the Land of the Outeniqua mountains, they found ample fresh water, forests teeming with game, and a rich and diverse sea life. It was, indeed, a land flowing with milk and honey, and it is no surprise that humans have thrived here, down through the ages.

Many of the historical sites do not appear in the text. Please refer to the maps, pages 120 - 127, and historical sites grid on page 134.

Victoria Bay in the early 1900s

PEOPLE OF THE STONE AGE

Unlike modern settlers who, in just three short centuries, plundered much of what Jan van Riebeeck had described as 'the finest forests in the world', Stone Age people lived in harmony with their surroundings.

Able to gather firewood for fuel, hunt game in the forests, and harvest nuts, berries and roots, they also found many caves in the area which provided shelter and warmth. As archaeologists have proved, the next million years would see a slow development of more sophisticated ways of harvesting the bounty of nature.

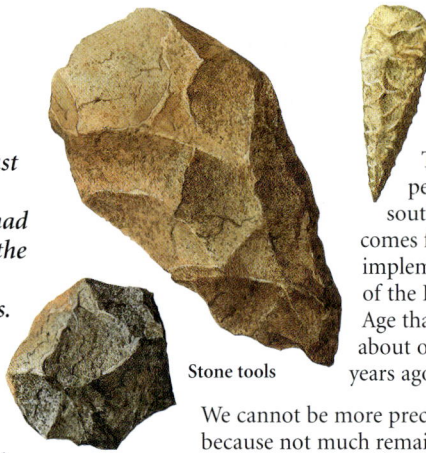

Stone tools

Earlier Stone Age

The earliest evidence of people living in the southern Cape comes from stone implements of the Earlier Stone Age that date back to about one million years ago.

We cannot be more precise because not much remains after such a long time. Usually it is only the stone tools that survive to show that people lived along the coast. There is no evidence that they ate fish and shellfish, although they certainly hunted game and ate wild plants.

Early Stone Age man

Early Stone Age people would have utilised forests like these for collecting food.

Collecting berries from the early forests

104

Nelson Bay Cave, rich with revealing middens

A great number of different shells have been found in middens all over this area.

Middle Stone Age

The history of people in the southern Cape is closely linked to global changes in sea level. This level rose and fell with melting and freezing of polar ice caps, in cycles that lasted about 100 000 years. About 125 000 years ago, when the climate was a little warmer and the sea level was higher than it is at present, Middle Stone Age people began enjoying shellfish as part of their diet. Piles of shells that were thrown away after the shellfish were eaten (shell middens) have been preserved in caves on the coast.

Shell middens that date from about 40 000 to 30 000 years ago, are now beneath the sea. This is because the sea level was lower then, and the coastline was as much as 100 km south of its present position. The colder climate at that time also led to some mammals having a larger body size. The bones of animals hunted by the people living inland show evidence of some 'giant' forms. For example, there were giant Cape horse / zebra and giant buffalo that were at least fifty percent larger than the similar modern species.

Later Stone Age

Fish gorges (hooks)

12 000 years ago, the sea level rose close to its present position.

Again there is plenty of evidence in the area of the activities of Later Stone Age people. Fishing and shellfish collecting, as well as hunting of small antelope, and collecting of ground game like tortoise and hare, were common. Later Stone Age people were the ancestors of the Khoesan and were technologically more advanced than the people of the Middle Stone Age. They made stone sinkers and bone points (or gorges) for fishing, and bows and arrows for hunting. They also made stone weights for sticks to help the women dig up roots, bulbs and corms.

Later Stone Age people were ancestors of the Khoesan.

Sinkers found at Nelson Bay Cave

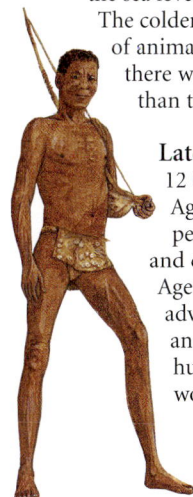

Hunter-Gatherers and Herders

The sea has been the centre of life in this area from the earliest times. The archaeological record shows that hunter-gatherers, living on the Southern Cape coast, used the sea as their main food source. The story of human settlement on this coast goes back at least 100 000 years. More recently, in the last 10 000 years, hunter-gatherers probably moved to the coast for the mild winter after spending the summer inland.

It was not until 2 000 years ago that people, who lived a different way of life from the hunter-gatherers, entered this area. Archaeologists have found evidence that, from that time, herding people used the southern Cape coast seasonally.

Hunter-gatherers

These people lived by hunting small mammals, and by fishing and gathering roots, bulbs and seeds. Archaeologists have found many artifacts that help us to understand how hunter-gatherers lived in this coastal area. There are a number of archaeological sites on the Garden Route that are easy to visit: Cape St. Blaize Cave at Mossel Bay which used to have a shell midden but has been largely destroyed (see site 7 on page 121); Nelson Bay Cave on the Robberg Peninsula (see site 31 on pages 125 and 126); and Matjes River Rock Shelter near Keurboomstrand (see site 39 on page 126). The fish traps at Still Bay and Rein's Coastal Nature Reserve (see sites 1 and 4 on page 120) are fascinating at low spring tide.

Shell pendants found at Nelson Bay Cave. Similar pendants have been found at the inland site of Melkhoutboom, north of Port Elizabeth.

Watsonia corms, page 69, an important food source.

Bored stone used as a weight when digging

Rock painting found in the area

Thou, O Tsui-Goa!
Thou father of the fathers!
Thou our father!
Let the thunder cloud stream!
Please let our flocks live!
Please let us also live!
I am so very weak indeed!
From thirst!
From hunger!
That I may eat field fruits!
Art thou not then our father?
The father of the fathers!
Thou Tsui Goa!
That we may praise thee!
That we may give thee in return! Thou father of the fathers! Thou our Lord!
Thou, O Tsui-Goa!

This is a hymn of praise to the Khoekhoe God Tsui-Goa! The hymn was first translated and recorded in the 1700s by Georges Schmidt, a missionary who came to work among the Khoekhoe. One of the field fruits mentioned in the hymn would have been Indian Grass. The bulb was collected by hunter-gatherers and herders and later by Dutch settlers who called them 'uintjies'.

Gatherer women collecting seeds and corms.

Painting tool

Fish traps (Still Bay), see sites 1 and 4 on page 120.

Artist's rendition
of a rock painting

Religion and Art

The area is rich in hunter-gatherer rock paintings. Most of these are in museums or on private land and are not accessible. The paintings of hunter-gatherers have a deep religious significance. They record their experiences of trances, which were important religious events. Like hunter-gatherers everywhere, those living along the southern Cape coast depicted animals in their trance paintings that were significant to their survival in that area. Certain animals, particularly the eland, were thought to be more powerful than others. The whale painting shown here is from a stone found near Storms River Mouth. The person 'swimming' with dolphins comes from a stone found at Klasies River Cave. Evidence of shellfish, fish caught with hooks and nets, seal bones and whale bones (probably from beached whales) show how much these people took advantage of the resources of the sea.

Herders

Hunter-gatherers kept sheep and cattle and moved to this coast from inland for the winter months. These people called themselves Khoekhoe (pronounced koi koi) which means 'men of men'. There is evidence of interaction between herder and hunter-gatherer societies. Herders sometimes relied on hunting, fishing and gathering to supplement their diet. Hunter-gatherers often worked as servants for the herders. Both groups also had contact with Xhosa Iron Age farmers who lived to the east, within the summer rainfall area, where their crops of sorghum and millet grew well.

One of the sources of evidence we have about these herding people are accounts and drawings made by travellers from Europe in the seventeenth and eighteenth centuries. Although these are not always accurate, because of the travellers' ignorance and prejudice, they do provide us with a rich source of evidence about the herders' way of life ...

"Their riches consist of cattle, such as oxen and sheep ...
If they will slaughter a beast they choose always the worst and thinnest, saying that it would be a pity to kill a fat animal".
Vermeulen, 1668, quoted in Raven-Hart, Major, R, Cape of Good Hope 1652-1702, the First Fifty years, 2 vols, Balkema, Cape Town, 1970.

Pottery shards

The Khoekhoe made pots like these for storing milk. Pieces of the pots can still be found in the area.

Distribution of herders in the seventeenth and eighteenth centuries

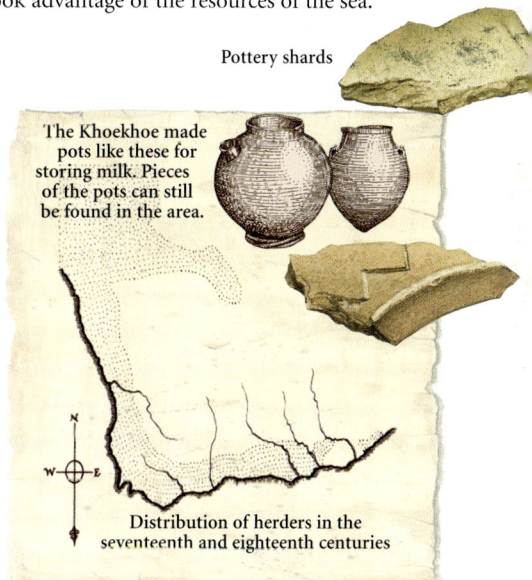
Koekhoe huts

"They have no houses but live in little huts which they make from bent sticks or hoops. They hang reed mats on the sticks. These huts are usually set ten or twelve together in a circle, within which their cattle stand by night, and by day roam widely round to graze. As soon as they see that their cattle have no more pasture, they take down their huts, lay the hoops on their pack oxen, and set them up elsewhere, wherever they find good grass."
Hoffmann, 1672, quoted in Raven-Hart, Major, R, Cape of Good Hope 1652-1702, the First Fifty years, 2 vols, Balkema, Cape Town, 1970.

TRAVELLERS AND SHIPWRECKS

The natural advantages of the coastal area included wide half-heart bays that made ideal harbours for passing ships. The fresh water and trade for meat with the Khoekhoe first brought the sea-faring European explorers on land. When the Dutch East India Company took over control of the trade route to the East, it set up a refreshment station at Cape Town in the seventeenth century. It was not long before travellers from the new settlement became aware of the riches of the southern Cape coast – today's Garden Route.

Portuguese travellers

The search for a sea passage from Europe to the East was the reason why Portuguese sailors passed this coast. In 1488 Bartolomeu Dias stopped to get fresh water at the place we call Mossel Bay today. A replica of his ship can be seen here in the Maritime Museum in the Bartolomeu Dias centre (see site 8 on page 121). Dias left the following account of his journey and of his meetings with the Khoekhoe herders ...

Dutch East India Company seal

"We sighted land in a bay which we called the Bahia dos Vaqueiros, because of the many cows seen there, watched by their herdsmen. And since they had no language which could be understood, we could have no speech with them; but rather they drove off their cattle inland, as if terrified of such a new matter, so that we could learn no more of them." Bartolomeu Dias, 1488, quoted in Raven-Hart, Major, R, Cape of Good Hope 1652-1702, the First Fifty years, 2 vols, Balkema, Cape Town, 1970.

17th Century navigational instrument

Replica of Bartholomeu Dias' ship

From this time onward many Portuguese ships stopped on their way to the East to collect water from the Hartenbos River that runs into Mossel Bay. They often traded beads and buttons for cattle and sheep with Khoekhoe herders.

Early sailors battling high seas

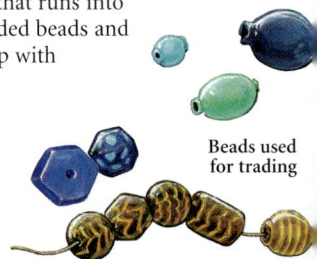

Beads used for trading

Shipwreck

White Milkwood (page 72)

The east coast of southern Africa was not safe for sailing ships and several Portuguese vessels sunk there in the fifteenth and sixteenth centuries. In 1630 the San Gonzales was on her way back to Portugal from India, when her captain stopped in the bay, called Plettenberg Bay today, to repair some leaks. Before the repairs could be done, the ship sank. 150 sailors drowned, but 100 swam to shore and lived in the Piesang Valley for eight months. While there, they built two boats with the remains of the San Gonzales and timber from the forest trees. One of the sailors left an account of their time on this coast ...

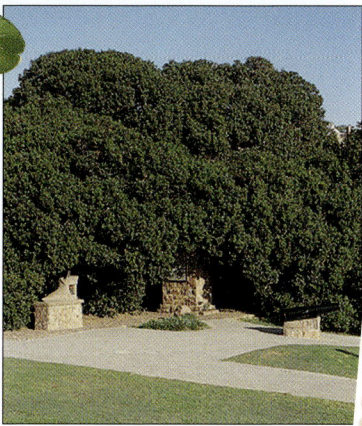

This White Milkwood was probably the first 'post office' on the southern Cape coast (see site 9 on page 121). In 1501 a Portuguese sailor João da Nova, found a letter left by another sailor in a boot hanging from this tree. The tree became known as the Post Office Tree. You can still see one of these trees in the same spot at Mossel Bay today.

"We built habitations of wood ... and sowed various seeds to enjoy the fruit thereof, such as pumpkins, melons, onions and coriander ... the soil is excellent, and free from stones, though there are various hills. These, as also the valleys, abound with verdure and plants with sweet smelling flowers. The trees are numerous and large. In all parts it is watered by voluminous rivers and abundant and fine springs ... There is an infinite number of wild animals of extraordinary size, such as deer, wolves, seals, buffaloes, wild boars, monkeys and also tigers and elephants."
Theal G M, Records of Southern Eastern Africa, 8 vols, Struik Reprint, Cape Town, 1964

Quill pen

The sailors eventually set out in the boats they had built, leaving behind a stone as a reminder of the original shipwreck. Known as the Van Plettenberg stone, it is housed in the Cape Town Museum, with a replica at Beacon Island, Plettenberg Bay (see site 36 on page 126). They were eventually picked up by other Portuguese vessels. Tragically, one of these ships sank with the shipwrecked sailors aboard, just as the ship entered the harbour at Lisbon.

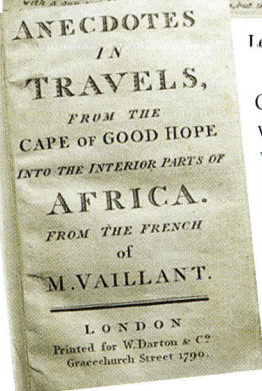

Travellers from Cape Town

Many travellers wrote accounts of their journey through this area. The most colourful account is perhaps that written by the Frenchman Le Vaillant.

ANECDOTES IN TRAVELS, FROM THE CAPE OF GOOD HOPE INTO THE INTERIOR PARTS OF AFRICA. FROM THE FRENCH of M.VAILLANT.

LONDON Printed for W.Darton & Cᵒ Gracechurch Street 1790.

Le Vaillant's book

One of the stories he tells is of his narrow escape with an elephant in the Knysna Forest. The wounded elephant charged him, and he escaped only by lying low on the ground. He and some Khoekhoe men then killed the elephant and, as this diary entry shows, made good use of the animal. This aimless hunting of the elephant continued well into the nineteenth century and eventually led to the animals' virtual extinction in the forest.

"We took such parts of the elephant as we wanted, particularly the fat, for greasing our wheels and traces and for burning. I had no cotton, and was obliged to make use of my cravats." Le Vaillant

Knysna Elephant, *Loxodonta africana*. Although elephants do not normally live in forests, hunting activities of the past forced those that remained into the Knysna Forest.

109

Nineteenth Century

Throughout the nineteenth century, people armed with the tools of the Industrial Revolution left Europe to find their fortunes on new continents. The natural advantages and resources of the Garden Route made it prime land for settlement and exploitation.

However, despite brief attempts at timber, gold and whaling, it never developed as a major urban or industrial area. This was because of the severe restrictions to travel presented by the deep gorges along the rivers, and the high ranges of the mountains running parallel to the coast.

Woodcutters in the Forest

In an age before oil wells and coal mines, timber was practically the only source of fuel available, so it was inevitable that the mighty forests lining the Garden Route were hungrily eyed by early settlers. Many hoped there would be easy money to be made in feeding this insatiable hunger for wood, and the first woodcutters were recorded at work in the forests in 1711. During the next two centuries, their numbers grew rapidly, even though most of them actually lived a poor and miserable existence, cut off from all civilisation. In spite of this, the woodcutters developed a strong cultural identity, and added a unique and distinctive flavour to the area. Indeed, it was not until 1939 that private woodcutting was finally banned altogether in the Outeniqua forests.

"The great bundles of logs were fastened together with chains, and attached to oxen. In front into the sea swam the touleier – a strong-swimming ox – while from behind other men drove the rest of the oxen … until they were alongside the boats and the logs loaded." "Plettenberg Bay to Knysna – a trip through history," in Kelley-Paterson, E., Looking Back, June 1971.

Black Stinkwood, (page 61)

Branches shown here are some of the tree species utilised by the woodcutters.

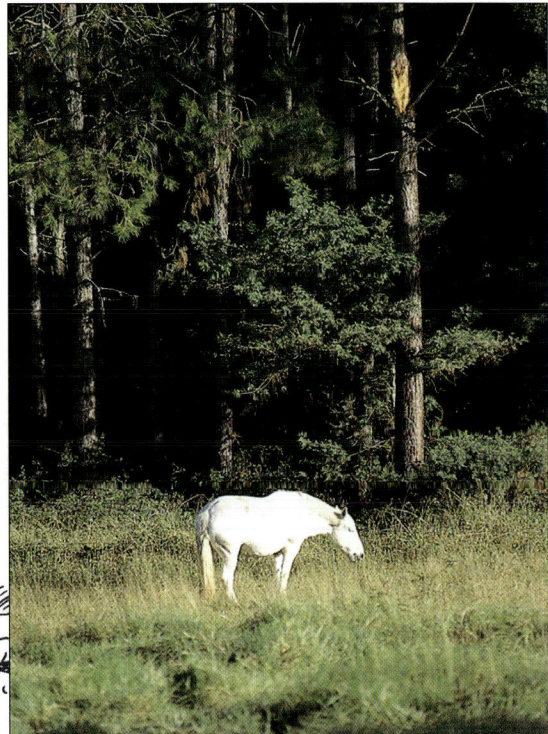

Percheron horses also dragged logs from the forest.

A woodcutters saw used in this period

Rock Ironwood (page 61)

*"The woods are very thick and produce
some of the tallest trees I ever beheld ...
The mountains are extremely steep and
many of the most stately trees grow out
of the naked strata of the rocks ...
These woods have their beginning to
the north of Mossel Bay and extend almost
120 miles to the east ending at a place
called Zitsicamma. Between the woods
and the Indian Ocean lies an extensive
plain inhabited by Europeans who traffic mostly
in wood which they bring in planks to the Cape."*
Lieutenant William Paterson, 1777, in Paterson,
W. Paterson's Cape Travels 1777-1779, ed.
Forbes V.S. and Rourke J, Brenthurst,
Johannesburg, 1980.

**Broad-leaved
Yellowwood
(page 61)**

Settlers

Off the main Knysna road
(see site 26 on page 124) you
will find a lone tombstone that
holds this inscription ..."In
memory of George Rex,
proprietor and founder of
Knysna." Rex is probably one of
the most famous of the settlers
who came to this area in the nineteenth century.
Legend claims that he was the son of George III of England and a
Quaker woman. Whether this is true or not, we know he arrived in
Knysna to settle on the farm Melkhoutkraal in 1804. He brought with
him his family, masons, carpenters, bricklayers, a blacksmith,
100 slaves and a plumber, all in 166 wagons.

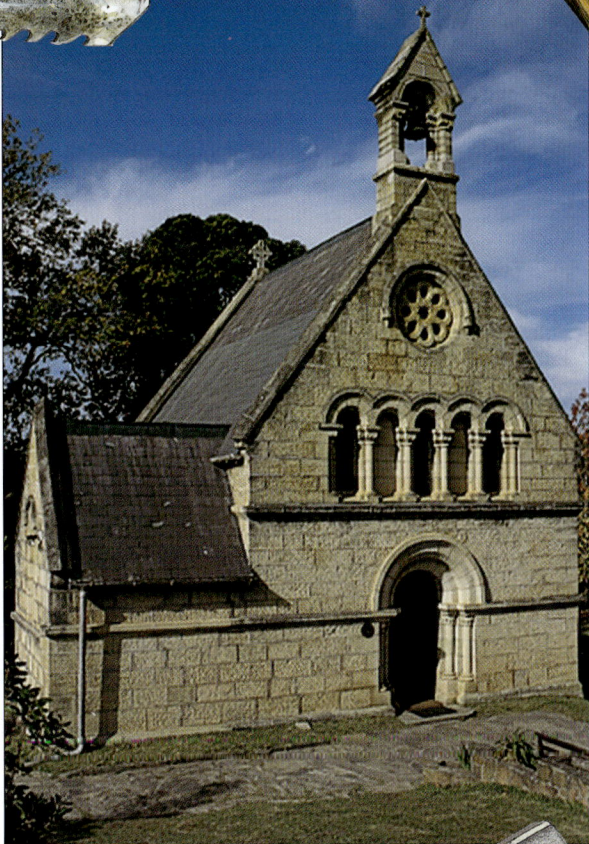

Belvidere Church

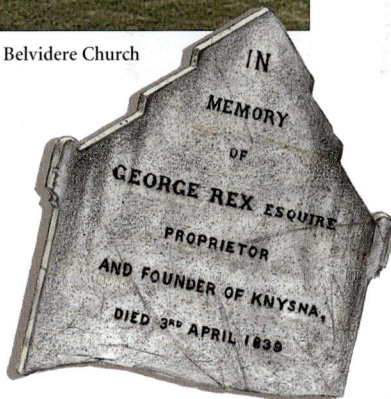

One of the best known landmarks left by Rex's family,
is the beautiful Belvidere Church consecrated in
1855 (see site 19 on page 124). The church was
built by Rex's son-in-law, Thomas Henry Duthie.
Duthie fell in love with Caroline Rex while
on a hunting expedition in the forest.
Duthie returned to settle at Belvidere where
he built the church and also the very beautiful
village of Knysna.

IN
MEMORY
OF
GEORGE REX ESQUIRE
PROPRIETOR
AND FOUNDER OF KNYSNA,
DIED 3RD APRIL 1839

George Rex's gravestone

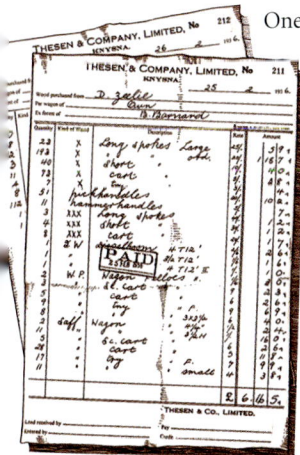

In 1869 another family, who had an important impact on the
area, arrived in Knysna. The Thesen family left Norway in their
ship the Albatross, on their way to settle in New Zealand.
They stopped in Knysna to deliver cargo and decided to
stay. The Thesens became involved in a number of business
activities, including shipping, commerce and timber.
To this day the name Thesen is associated with timber
in the Knysna area.

**Small-leaved
Yellowwood
(page 61)**

Documents from Thesen's
Company, from the early 1900s

111

Nineteenth and Twentieth Centuries

As the nineteenth century progressed, settlers continued to be drawn by the promise of a better life in the furthest reaches of the African continent. Towns like Plettenburg Bay and Knysna were established, and while they would never play a major role in South Africa's economic development, the prosperity of the area was assured.

Gold nuggets

Sifting pan used by the diggers

The Forests

The increasing demand for timber began to threaten the forests, and as early as 1803, the traveller Lichtenstein warned of the serious depletion of the indigenous trees ...

"Even here, the timber begins so far to fail that whereas formerly they did not cut any for beams less than 30 feet high, none are now found except in the deep kloof." Lichtenstein, 1803, in Lichtenstein, H, Travels in Southern Africa, 1803, 1804, 1805, 2 vols, Van Riebeeck Society, Cape Town, VRC 10/11, 1928, 1930

Felled alien trees

The Great Fire

Disaster struck the forest in 1869 when a great fire raged for weeks from Mossel Bay to Humansdorp. After the fire, the only trees that remained were those growing in the deep kloofs. It was only now that the authorities began to consider the conservation of the forests. The first conservator was appointed in 1874, and in 1880, a French forestry expert made a misguided attempt to conserve the forest. Although he stopped the felling of trees in some areas, he also planted many exotic species including pines and gums. These alien trees overran the indigenous vegetation and, today, over a century later, efforts to clear these aliens are still ongoing in many areas.

Cluster Pine (page 117)

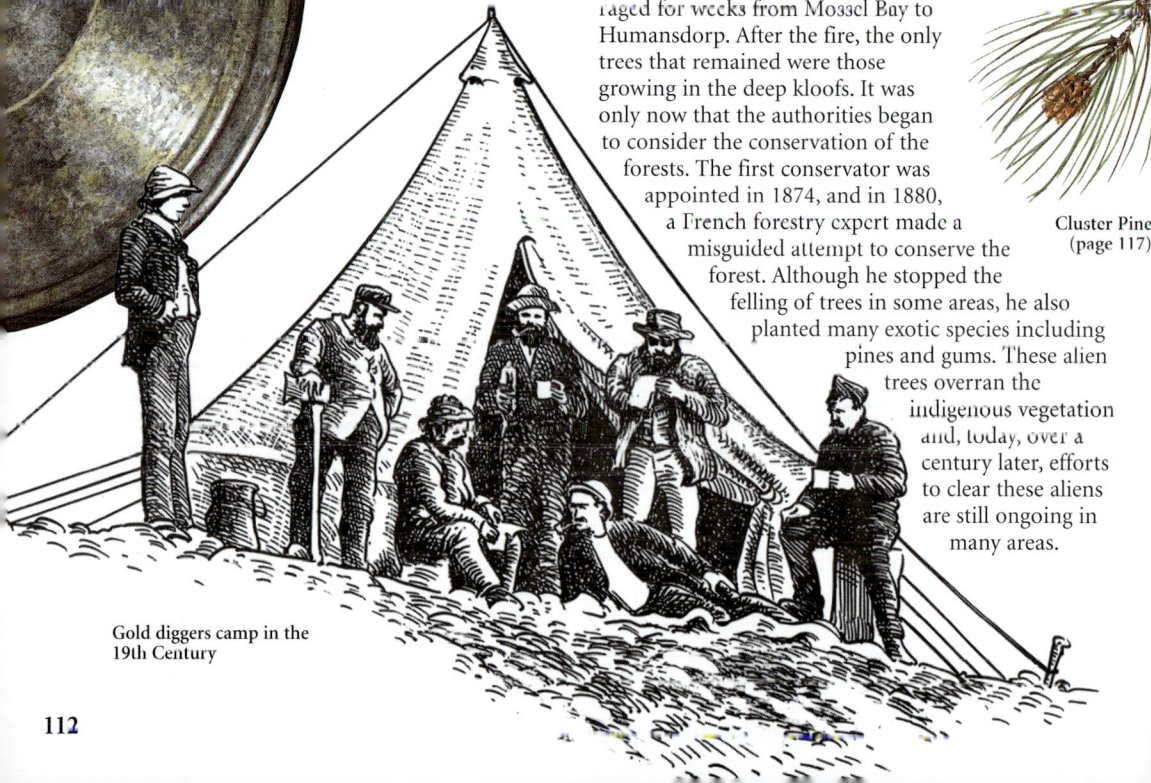

Gold diggers camp in the 19th Century

Diggers, Whalers and the Railway

It was not only timber that drew people to the southern Cape Coast. There was gold too! In 1876, a gold nugget was found at Millwood in the Knysna forest. Diggers from all over the world arrived to find their fortunes in the forests. By 1888, a small town had grown at Millwood, but no great goldfields were found. When news of the gold-finds on the Reef came to this area, most of the diggers left, and Millwood became a ghost town. Visit the site of the town today and you will find an old building, Monks' Store, and signs to indicate where the streets once were. Close to the town in the forest are old mine shafts and machinery hidden now in the dense undergrowth.

Millwood Museum

Early whaling off the Cape coast

Apart from wood and gold from the forests, modern settlers also tried to take advantage of other riches of the area. In 1912, a Norwegian whaling company set up a whaling station at Beacon Island (see site 32 on page 126). From here the boats set out into the Indian Ocean in search of the Southern Right Whale that frequents these waters. Whaling operations stopped in 1916. Since the moratorium on whaling was instituted in 1983, the whale population has increased world-wide by about 7% each year.

Brass number plate of the Outeniqua steam train

The inaccessibility of the area continued to prevent many people from exploring the coast and forests. It was only when the railway line was built, that more visitors frequented the southern Cape. In 1928, a railway line from George to Knysna was completed. You can relive the excitement of this moment by travelling the same line on the steam train, the Outeniqua Choo-tjoe (see site 22 on page 124).

Outeniqua Choo-tjoe

113

HUMAN IMPACT

Humans are as much a part of the environment as any other living organism. However, we are the most destructive. Many natural areas of South Africa are under threat from the increase in human activities – from recreational to commercial – and the Garden Route is no exception. The following information will help you to preserve this spectacular part of the country, and to minimize your impact on the area.

Fires

Natural fires, such as those caused by lightning, play a role in shaping the landscape. Unnatural, runaway fires during the hot, dry summers can devastate the environment. If you wish to light fires for picnicking purposes, do so only in designated places, and be sure to extinguish them when you leave.

Many fynbos plants, like the King Protea (page 67) need natural fires, in the correct season to enable regeneration.

Fires are a natural occurence, unless started by humans.

Buy your own wood for making fires. Collecting of firewood in natural areas, including forests and dunes, is prohibited. Dead wood forms an important part of the food-web and is home to many small creatures.

Rhinoceros Beetles (page 79) use decomposing vegetation as breeding sites, and are important in the natural cycle.

Excessive use of recreational areas can have a detrimental effect on the environment, for example overfishing. Please clean up after visiting, so that you don't harm the wildlife, and so that others may enjoy the Garden Route after you.

Litter

Human activity generates an enormous amount of litter that is not only potentially hazardous to wildlife and people, but also spoils the natural beauty of the environment. Before you throw your litter on the ground, consider that it takes 100 to 400 years for glass to disintegrate, and up to 30 years for plastic to decompose! If there are no bins provided in the area, please take your litter with you and consider recycling it.

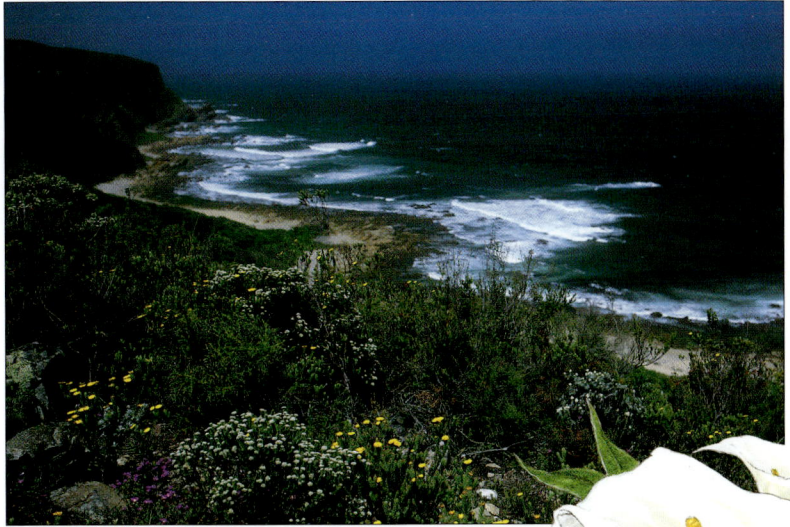

This unique beauty is worthy of our care

Ground disturbance

Specially constructed paths and roadways have been created in many areas to protect the natural vegetation and wildlife from destruction, and to decrease soil erosion. When walking, hiking or driving, please stick to demarcated areas to avoid destroying sensitive plants, animals and soil. Picking of plants along public roads and in nature reserves is prohibited. Flowers are the sex organs of plants that create the next generation. So admire them, but don't pick them.

Picking flowers, like the Arum Lily (page 65), spoils the natural beauty and destroys the habitats of other living creatures, like the Arum Lily Frog (page 85).

Ancient History

If you are visiting areas with rock paintings, archaeological sites or other historical monuments, please consider them part of your natural heritage. To deface or remove any part of these ancient implements is a crime and spoils them for future generations.

Rock painting of a San woman with a digging 'stick' (page 106).

Offroad Vehicles and Power Boats

These forms of recreation are very popular in South Africa. However, their impact on the environment can be devastating. Water pollution, noise pollution and the destruction of natural terrain can permanently damage plant and animal life. Please be sure to familiarise yourself with the guidelines and regulations before entering natural areas.
Enjoy, but don't destroy our Garden Route!

Natural foodchains are dependant on a healthy, pollution-free environment, for example the White Steenbras (page 49) that feeds on prawns in estuaries.

Boating and flyfishing on Knysna Lagoon

Sand Prawn (page 53)

115

HUMAN IMPACT

ALIEN ANIMALS AND PLANTS

An alien species is a plant or animal which does not naturally occur in a defined area but which has been introduced from elsewhere by humans. An invasive (invader) species is usually an alien plant or animal which is capable of displacing indigenous species and causing irreversible changes. This is because there are no natural predators or control measures so it can reproduce and spread more rapidly.

In many areas, invasive alien plants such as pines, Hakeas and Acacias, dominate the natural fynbos vegetation in the southern Cape.

Fynbos is the most water-efficient vegetation type, and therefore allows maximum water to run-off into dams and rivers. Most aliens use enormous amounts of water and therefore limit species diversity and reduce the amount of water run-off considerably. Because of the aliens and the growing human population, a serious shortage of water is predicted for the future in this area.

◄ **Argentine Ant**
Linepithema humile Insect (3 mm)
The Argentine Ant invades areas of fynbos. Unlike indigenous ants, they eat oily parts of the seeds on the soil-surface, leaving the seeds exposed and vulnerable. Re-generation of those plants that depend on ants becomes much less successful. It may even result in certain species being threatened with extinction.

◄ **Common Starling (European Starling)**
Sturnus vulgaris
Bird (20 - 22 cm) 757
A cocky, quarrelsome bird that was introduced to Cape Town by Cecil John Rhodes in 1899, and is now well established in the southern Cape. It inhabits urban areas and farmyards where it often occurs in flocks of hundreds. It is generally disliked because it tends to displace other birds from town gardens and carries lice and mites. The Common Starling feeds on fruit, seeds, insects and food-scraps discarded by humans.

◄ **Largemouth Bass**
Micropterus salmoides
Fish (60 cm)
Originally from North America, these fish were introduced as popular freshwater gamefish. They have caused lots of damage to indigenous fish populations.

Mosquito Fish ►
Gambusia affinis
Fish (6 cm)
Originally from North America, these fish were introduced for mosquito control and as food for bass. As they feed on larvae of other fish, they are threatening indigenous fish populations.

▼ **Mozambique Tilapia**
Oreochromis mossambicus
Fish (40 cm)
Introduced to the southern Cape from south-east Africa, these fish live in rivers, lakes, lagoons and estuaries. They feed mainly on algae, and dead plant material.

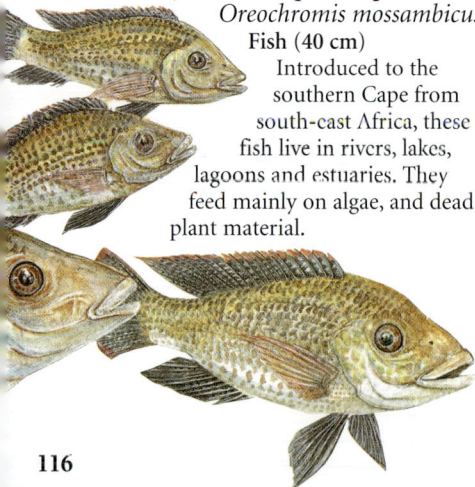

Bluegill Sunfish ►
Lepomis macrochirus
Fish (20 cm)
Originally from North America, these fish were introduced as fodder fish for bass. They are now a serious pest as they compete with indigenous fish.

116

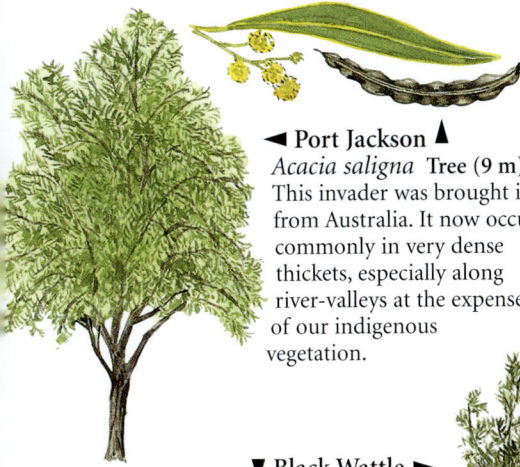

◄ **Port Jackson** ▲
Acacia saligna **Tree (9 m)**
This invader was brought in from Australia. It now occurs commonly in very dense thickets, especially along river-valleys at the expense of our indigenous vegetation.

Rooikrans ►
Acacia cyclops
Tree (3 - 5 m)
An unwelcome bushy tree that has narrow leaves and small, yellow flowers. Its seed-pods are coiled and the seeds, red with black centres, look like 'red eyes'. It was introduced from Australia, and grows in dense thickets which invade the indigenous vegetation.

▼ **Black Wattle** ►
Acacia mearnsii **Tree (10 m)**
The unwelcome Black Wattle has black, stringy bark, dark-green, feathery leaves and small, yellow flowers. It was introduced from Australia for the commercial use of its bark in the tanning industry. It now forms dense stands along river valleys throughout the southern Cape. This makes it difficult for indigenous plants to grow.

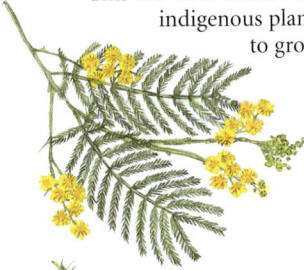

Blue Gum ▼
Eucalyptus globulus
Tree (70 m)
The Blue Gum was introduced to South Africa in 1828. The bark was traditionally used for timber, fuel, windbreaks, shade and ornaments. It was once planted extensively, but has however been superseded by species which are faster-growing and more resistant to fungus and insect attack. Noble, giant specimens still remain throughout the country as landmarks of early settlers.

◄ **Silky Hakea**
Hakea sericea
Tree (2,5 m)
This invader is an erect, single-stemmed shrub. Brought in from Australia, infestations now occur on all the major coastal ranges in the southern Cape. It poses a threat to the unique mountain fynbos which it smothers entirely. Conservation organisations spend millions of rands annually in an attempt to bring this plant under control.

◄ **Cluster Pine** ▼
Pinus pinaster **Tree (30 m)**
Pine trees were introduced to South Africa for their valuable soft wood. The Cluster Pine, introduced from the Mediterranean countries, has 'escaped' from plantations and is now threatening the natural plants growing in the southern Cape.

Maps and Activities

The "Garden Route" is a marketing concept to promote the beauty of this fragile narrow strip of extraordinary coastline from Still Bay to Storms River.

The following maps will provide you quick and easy reference. They are colour-coded, and are cross-referenced on the activity grids on pages 128 – 141. For the key to road map signs see Map One, page 120.

These maps have undergone extensive research and testing. However, the publisher welcomes any comments and information from the public that could help to improve and/or correct the content.

The following terms are common on signposts along the Garden Route:

Afrikaans	English
Berg	Mountain
Rivier	River
Baai	Bay
Mond	Mouth
Strand	Beach
Groot	Great, Large
Klein	Little, Small
Woud	Forest
Punt	Point
Boom	Tree
Brug	Bridge
Tuin	Garden
Wildtuin	Game Reserve/ National Park

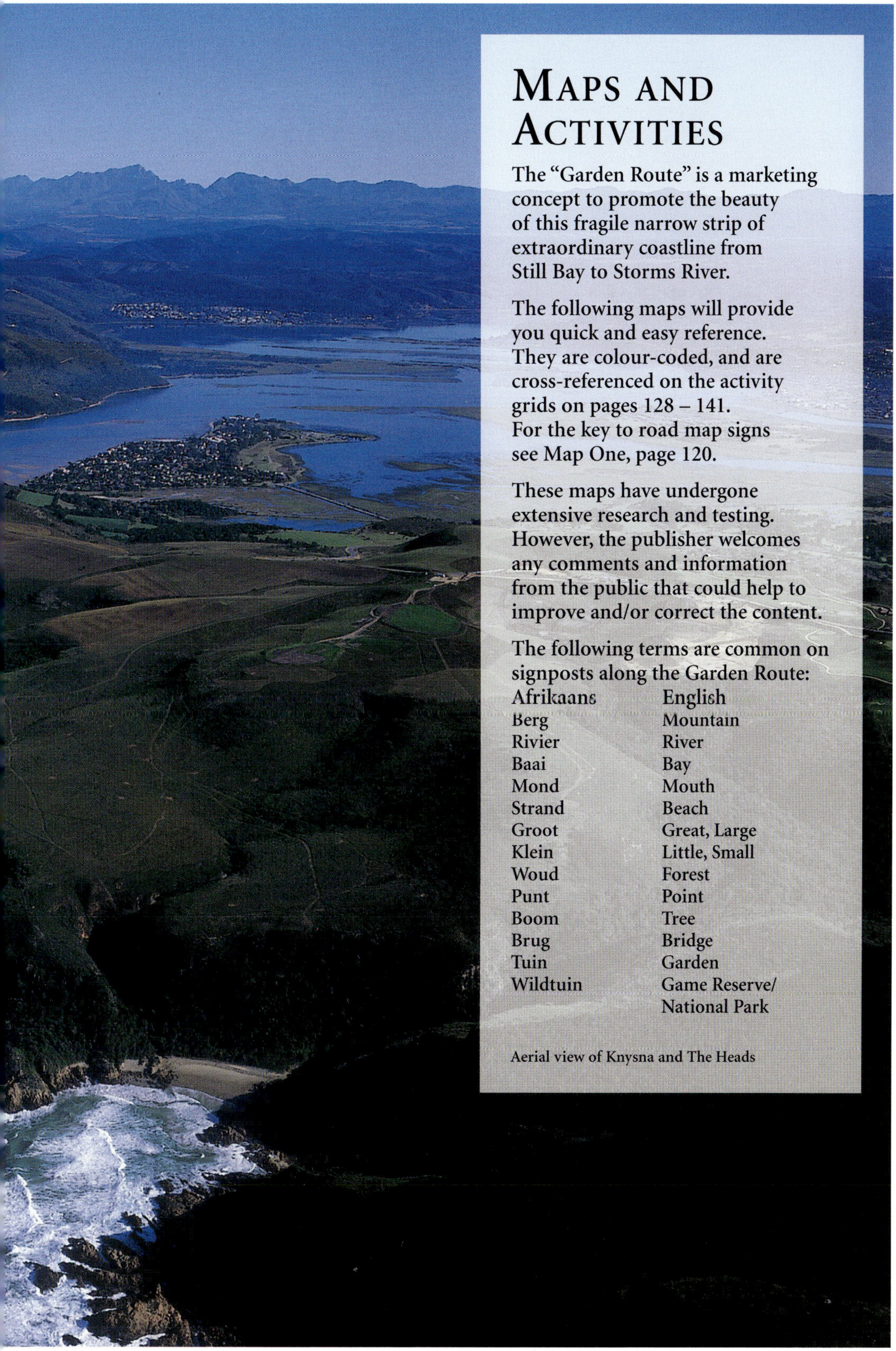

Aerial view of Knysna and The Heads

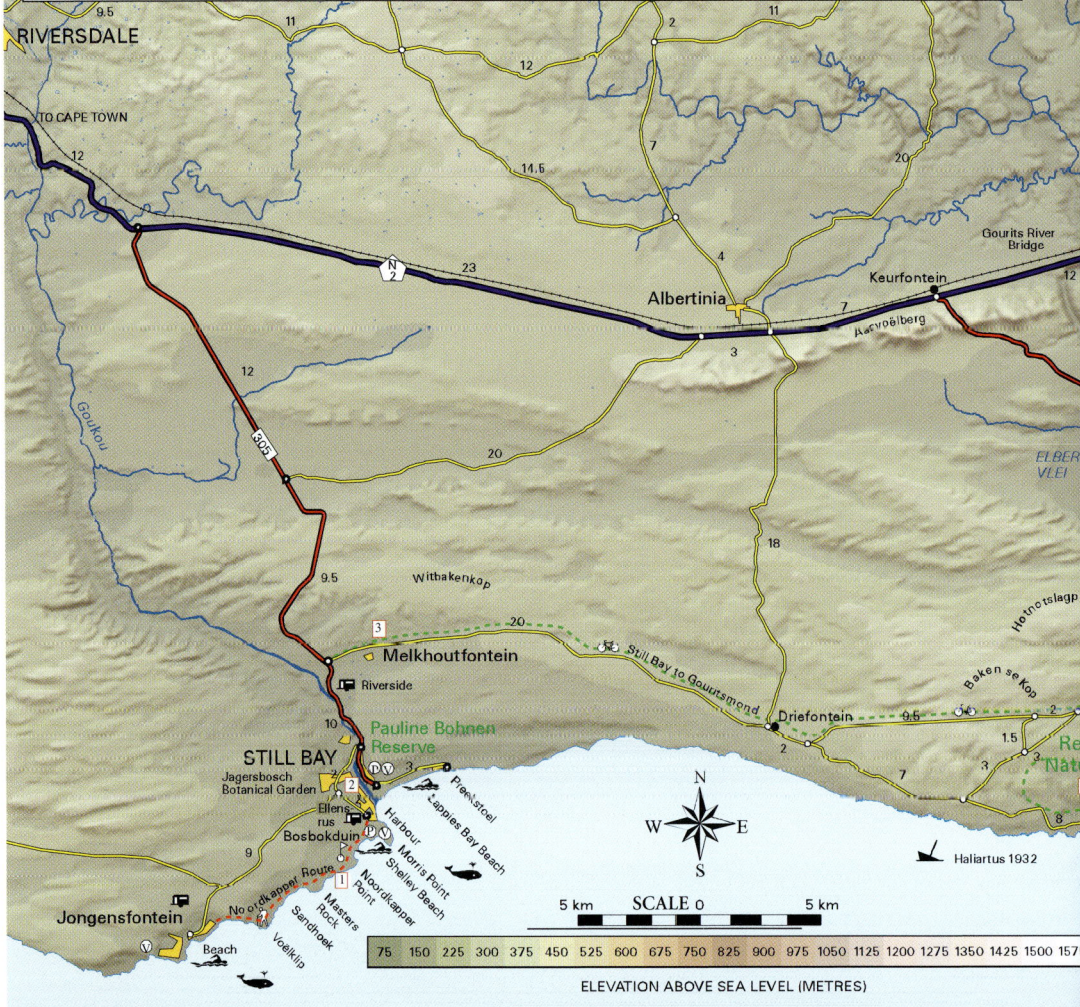

MAP ONE

STILL BAY TO GREAT BRAK RIVER

Scenically tranquil, the coastal plain from Still Bay to
Mossel Bay is wide, with big, meandering rivers. Here
there is less influence of a large inland mountain
range until north of the Hartenbos River, where the
Outeniquas dominate the landscape. Mossel Bay is the
largest bay and harbour (shown here) along the coast.

KEY TO MAP SYMBOLS

Town or Large Settlement	Siding	Bathing Beach	Golf Course
Village or Small Settlement	Airport	Whale Watching	Caravan Park
National Road	River	Dive Site	2 Historical Site
325 Main Road	Dam, Lake or Lagoon	Ship Wreck	Arts and Crafts
Secondary Road	Marine Reserve	Viewpoint	Hiking or Walking Trail
5 Distance Markers (Kilometres)	Picnic Site	Information Centre	Hiking Trail Hut
Railway Line			Cycle Trail

RIVERSDALE

9.5   11   2   11

12

TO CAPE TOWN

12

14.6

N2   23

Albertinia

Keurfontein

Gourits River Bridge

7

4

20

12

3

7   Aasvoëlberg

12

ELBER VLEI

20

18

Hotnetslagp

9.5   Witbakenkop

3   20   Still Bay to Gouritsmond

Melkhoutfontein

Riverside   Driefontein   9.5

Baken se Kop

1.5

Pauline Bohnen Reserve   2

Re Nat

10

STILL BAY
Jagersbosch Botanical Garden   2   3   Preekstoel

Ellens rus
Bosbokduin   Harbour   Lappies Bay Beach   7   3

9   Morris Point

Noordkapper Route   1   Shelley Beach   8

Jongensfontein   Masters Rock   Noordkapper Point

Haliartus 1932

Sandhoek   Voëlklip

Beach

N
W E
S

5 km   SCALE 0   5 km

| 75 | 150 | 225 | 300 | 375 | 450 | 525 | 600 | 675 | 750 | 825 | 900 | 975 | 1050 | 1125 | 1200 | 1275 | 1350 | 1425 | 1500 | 157 |

ELEVATION ABOVE SEA LEVEL (METRES)

OUTENIQUA
MTNS

Outeniqua
Nature
Reserve

JONKERSBERG
PLANTATION

NGEBERG

Robinson
Pass

Eight Bell
Mountain
Inn Hike

1.5

10

15

*Wolwedans
Dam*

10

7.5

14

8.5

Palmiet

328

16

Ossie's
Game
Ranch

1

4.5

P

V

7

5

5

rtsdale

Great
Brak River

The
Great Brak

Imbabala
Game Farm

GEELBEKVLEI

Little
Brak River

7

9.7

3

4

3

Reebok

Tergniet Beach

13

327

Hartebeeskuil Dam

6

3

Botlierskop
Game Farm

5

Little Brak Beach

Hartenbos

3

Little Brak Beach

13

8

3

HARTENBOS
Hartenbos Beach

11

8

9

Seal
Island

Dias Beach
Die Bakke
Madiba Beach

Die Bergies

8

MOSSEL BAY

Bartlesfontein

Mossel Bay Harbour Wall
Romanshank Rocks

11

Kleinberg

Mosgas

9

10

Die Punt

Cooper Lin de se Berg

N
2

KWANONQABA

16

S

Die Poort & Cape
St. Blaize Lighthouse
Cape St. Blaize
Okkuidrots
Tonnelgrotte

4.5

6

5

4

Cape St. Blaize Trail

13

DANA BAY

Pinnacle Point

14

9.5

Vleesbaai - Dana Bay Beach Walk

VOELVLEI

I N D I A N   O C E A N

Johnson's
Post

Boggomsbaai

Vleesbaai Beach

6

2

4.5

Vleesbaai

325

1

Vleespunt
Fransmanshoek

Rooibankies

6

Cannon Beach
Cannon Point

stal
rve

Cycle Route

Gourits River Mouth
Gourits Beach

P

V

Gouritsmond

12

Bank

Cape Mountain Zebra
(vulnerable species)
Equus zebra zebra (II. 1,3 m; 245 kg)
On the brink of extinction in the early 1900s, with
less than 100 individuals remaining, these animals
have made a remarkable recovery through sound
conservation efforts. A small population at Rein's
Coastal Nature Reserve has been re-introduced,
into an area where they were once abundant.

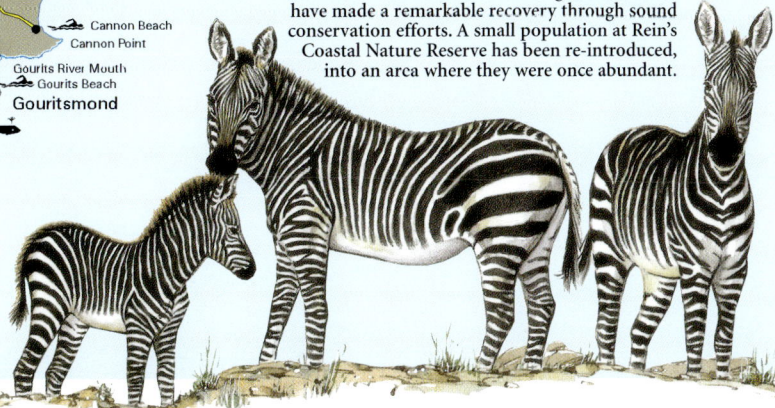

MAP TWO

GLENTANA TO SEDGEFIELD

The Map of South Africa, Wilderness (shown here) is part of the magnificent Outeniqua range. This range and numerous small rivers and a string of amazingly varied lakes are enough to create a holiday paradise. Being along a fifty kilometre stretch of cliffs, boulders and carved-out beaches on the mighty Indian Ocean is added eco-holiday joy.

GEELHOUTBOOMBERG

OUTENIQUA MNTS

OUTENIQUA MNTS

TO OUDTSHOORN

N 12

19

Outeniqua Nature Reserve

Pass to Pass Trail

Montagu Pass Route

Outeniqua Pass

Montagu Pass

Cradock Peak

Melville Peak

George Peak

Craddock/George Peak Trail

Tierkop Trail

Tierkop

Tierkop

Groen Kop

Cradock Pass Trail

Jonkersberg Plantation

Witfontein Forest Station

Witfontein Walk

BLANCO

2.5

4

3.5

12/13

Garden Route Dam

Kat

Tierkop Trail

Groenewelde Forest

Saasveld

Fancourt

George

GEORGE

Seven Passes Road

15

Geelhoutboom Trail

8

WITELS RIVER VLEI

Garden Route Dam

Outeniqua Railroad/ Choo-tjoe

4.5

N 12

Map of Africa

5

4

6

102

Thembaletu

Victoria Bay

Le Kli

VOELVLEI

George

Gwaing

Gwaing

Schaapkop

Ballots Bay Nature Reserve

Ballots Bay

Keanm Mou River Bay Victoria Bay Beach

102

N 2

14

PACALTSDORP

Mission Rd

Rooikransies

Bloubank

Skuinsbank

MOSSEL BAY

Outeniqua

Madjigala

Glentana

Glentana Beach Walk

Ghwano Bay

Voelklip Walk

Rooikransies

Voelklip

Duttons Cove Walk

Scotts Bank

The Point

Herolds Bay Beach

Vaalkom

Gwaing River Mouth

Oubaai (Duttons Cove)

Preekstoel

Rooiklip Jacobs Point

INDIAN OCEAN

Glentana

11

Glentana Beach

1902

Cape Windlass

Herolds Bay

Leopard (vulnerable species)
Panthera pardus (H: 60 - 75 cm)
Leopards are an endangered species due to persecution by stock farmers. They are, however, important in controlling numbers of so-called problem animals, such as baboons and caracal. They are not confined by man-made fences, and so it is difficult to create safe refuges in which to conserve them.

Perdekop
Windmeulnek
Outeniqua Trail
Langbos

Bergplaas Plantation
Van der Wattsbos
Karatara
Karatara Pass

Bergplaas
Beervlei Indigenous Forest
Old Knysna / George Road

Woodville Forest
Hoogekraal Pass
1.5
3

Woodville
Start of Outeniqua Trail
11
Hoekraal

Woodville Big Tree
6.5
Beervlei

5
1
Duiwe
8

Diep

6
Forest Road
louws

6
6
9

Hoekville
Kingfisher Trails

erness eights
Wilderness National Park

5.5
Ebb & Flow
Vlei Sand Road
14

Island Lake
LANGVLEI
Cape Dune Molerat Trail
SWARTVLEI

3.5
1.5
RONDE-VLEI
3
Ruigtvlei
Ruigtevlei

WILDERNESS
2.5
2
4
9
N2
Bleshoender Hoek
Montmere
TO KNYSNA
4

WILDERNESS LAGOON
Flat Rock
Klein Krantz
Klein Krantz Gerickes Walk
1
Outeniqua Railroad / Choo-tjoe
7.5
2

ss Beach
Wilderness Dune Beach
Wilderness N P
2.5
SEDGEFIELD
GROENVLEI

Swartvlei Beach Walk
Sedgefield Beach
Myoli Beach
Groenvlei Bush Camp

Gerickes Point
Swartvlei Beach
SWARTVLEI LAGOON
Goukamma Nature Reserve
Platbank No. 1

N
W E
S

5 km

123

MAP THREE

GOUKAMMA TO PLETTENBERG BAY

Renowned for its nearby mountains, forests, human history and lagoon, the Knysna area has been a lifestyle and tourist destination for over a century. Holiday-makers return to the same spots decade after decade, especially to the Knysna Heads (western head shown here).

TO UNIONDAL VIA PRINCE ALRED'S PAS

Haarlbos   Outeniqua Trail

Jubilee Creek Nature Reserve

Milkwood Mine Walk

Jubilee Creek Walk

18

Buffelsnek Plantation

Kraaibos

Outeniqua Route

Marais Kop

Outeniqua Rou

Homtini Route   Portland Heights

Krisjan se Nek Route

Goudeveld Indigenous Forest

Knysna

Outeniqua Trail

Lelievlei Nature Reserve

Rondebossie

Terblans Walk

Jonkersberg   Outeniqua

atara

Barrington

13.5

11

Goudeveld Forest Station

Keurhoek

Roolels

Gouna Indigenous Forest

Gouna

Homtini

Homtini Pass   Rheenendal

17   Portland Manor Estate

19

Gouna

Steenbr

8

G E O Parkes & Sons Indigenous Forest and Plantation

Spioenkop

Phantom Pass

7

Simold

Old Cape Road

Bergplaas Plantation

Grootkops

339

Groot

Outeniqua Railroad / Choo-tjoe

GROENVLEI

8.5

N2

3

5

4.5

3

2.5

The Indiger Fo and Planta

2.5

5

1

3.5

Pledge Nature Reserve

KNYSNA   ℹ

2.5

5

Vlei Camp

Goukamma Nature Reserve

19

Belvidere

6.5

Brenton on Lake

2

Waterfront Drive

20/22

Thesen's Island

26

Monks

4

Hornlee

6

KNYSNA LAGOON

Knysna Golf Course

Leisure Island

WOODBOURNE PAN

Sparrebe

Goukamma Beach

Goukamma Beach Walk

Brenton Beach Walk

Brenton on Sea

23

Featherbed Nature Reserve

24

Woodbourne

Barview Crescent

25

Goukamma River Mouth

Buffelsbaai

Castle Rock   Brenton Beach

The Heads   Coney Glen Beach

Knoetzie

Knoetze b

Walker's Bay   Rooiwehoek   Walker Point

N
W   E
S

0   5 km

INDIAN OCEAN

Brenton Blue
(threatened species
& endemic)
Orachrysops niobe
(19 - 32 mm)

(M)

The Brenton Copper
butterflies are extremely
rare and endangered, and are
only found at Brenton-on-Sea.
They have a close relationship with
the Cock-tail Ant. The ant feeds on
secretions from the honey gland, and
in return the ants protect the larvae.
The Brenton Blue butterflies only occur
at Brenton-on-Sea Reserve.

(M)

Brenton Copper
(threatened
species and endemic)
Chrysoritis mithras (24 - 28 mm)

Under-side

Tarkaberg

Palmiet

Diep

Kruisvallei

Jakkalskraal Mnts

Malvarug

Spitskop

11

339

8

Wynandskraal Mnts

Keurbooms

Keurboomsriver
Plantation

Buffelsnek
Forest Station

340

Ysternek
Nature Reserve

9

Kransbos
Forest Station

Whiskey Creek
Nature Reserve

Hartbees

1.5

The Elephant
Trails

3

Rondebos

Buffelsnek
Plantation

15

Keurbooms River
Nature Reserve

2.5 Diepwalle
Forest Station

Bitou

Diepwalle
Indigenous Forest

TO
STORMS
RIVER

Petrus se Brand Cycle Trail

Outeniqua Trail

San
Marino

7

Fisantehoek

Bitou

Wittedrift

340

5

N2

2

Knysna
Elephant Park

Stanley's
Island

Dune
Park

Keurbo
Beach

6

Garden
of Eden

Bitou

Wittedrift Trails

4

7

Goose
Valley

N2

3.5

4

Breeding Colony

Harkerville

1

2.5

6

4.5

New
Horizons

KEURBOOMS
LAGOON

Brackenhill
Falls

Forest Station

Kwanakhatula

2

Lookout Beach
Lookout Rocks

Harkerville Routes

Kranshoek

20

32-38

The Wedge
Hobie Beach

Piesang Valley

1.5

Sinclair
Nature Reserve

Harkerville Forest

Harkerville Trails

8.5

Piesang

Plettenberg
Bay

Central Beach
Beacon Island Rocks
Robberg Beacon Island Beac

Sinclair

Kranshoek Trail

5

3.5

PLETTENBERG BAY

Groot
Kop

Romansgat

2

27

Kranshoek

1.5

Plettenberg
Bay

28

Robberg 5

Stevens Bank

Rookkrans

Nelson Bay

Platbank No. 2

Ghwanopad

Stilbaai

Plettenberg
Bay

2

1.5

30

Robberg
Corner

Merile Bank
The Gap
Kanon Koeël Gat

3

31

Robberg Trails

Robberg
Nature
Reserve

The Island

Island
Beach

The Point

The Ledge
Whale Rock

MAP FOUR

KEURBOOMSSTRAND TO STORMS RIVER

Arguably the most beautiful part of the Garden Route, the world famous Plettenberg Bay and Keurbooms Lagoon make this coastal stretch South Africa's premier holiday resort with all the facilities that this entails. Despite this, the true outdoor-lover has literally thousands of venues to explore far from the human noise and bustle, like the De Vasselot Nature Reserve (shown here).

Die Korsyn Trail

Witberg

Klein Benekop

Tsitsikamma Trail

Bobbejaans

Groot

Bloukrans

Blaauwkrantz

Bloukrans

Bekenkop

Grenas Ca

Keurbooms Forest Station

Redford

2

Bloukrans Forest

12

Bloukrans State Forest Station

Lotterin Plantati

Whiskey Creek Nature Reserve

6.5

Kurland

1.5

De Vasselot Nature Reserve

8

102

Bloukrans Pass

42

Vark

The Crags

Stinkhoutkloof Trail

Tsitsikamma Trail

Cold

16

Monkeyland

7

10

De Vasselot

3

3.5

Bloukrans Rest Area & Tsitsikamma Forest Village

11

Lily Pond

Kalender

41

Groot Kloof Trail

Marine Drive

Bloukrans Bridge

10

Hog Hollow

N 2

Matjies

Natures Valley Trail

NATURE'S VALLEY

Andre

2.5

Otter Trail

Otter Trail

TO PLETTENBERG BAY

Forest Hall

40

Keurbooms-strand

Keurbooms Matjies River Walk

39

Arch Rock

Picnic Rock

Keurbooms Beach

Cathedral Rock

Grootbank Platbank No. 3

Salt River Mouth

Blue Rocks

Main Beach

Die Punt

Groot River Mouth

Klip River Mouth

Bloukrans River Mouth

Tsitsikam

4

Eastern Cape Redfin Minnow (threatened species)
Pseudobarbus afer (11 cm)
Eastern Cape Redfin is endemic to the coastal rivers of this area. Populations of this minnow are being threatened by alien fish (such as bass and trout) and their associated parasites, water extraction and alien plant infestation. The Eastern Cape Redfin attains its beautiful red colouration during the breeding season. Redfins as a group are highly threatened, and are unique to the southern tip of Africa.

N
W E
S

0   5 km

For the key to road map signs see Map One (page 120). These maps have undergone extensive research and testing. However, the publisher welcomes any comments and information from the public that could help to improve and / or correct the content.

Noekop

Spitskop

TSITSIKAMMA WILDERNESS COMPLEX

Camel Pile

Heidekop

Tsitsikamma Trail

Keurbos

Tsitsikamma Trail

Heuningbos

Lottering

Elandsbos Forest

Elandsbos

Kleinbos

Storms river

Tsitsikamma Trail

Sleepkloof

Storms

Witteklip Forest

43

Big Tree P

Tsitsikamma Total Village

102

1.5

1

STORMS RIVER

4

8.5

Forest Station

Storms River Forest

Witteklip

Storms River Pass

45

TO PORT ELIZABETH

N 2

8

Oakhurst

Otter Trail

8

P Old Bridge

Bloubos

1.5

2

ational Park

Elandsbos River Mouth

Scott

Blue Bay

Skilder Krans

Ngubu

Otter Trail

Storms River Mouth

44

V P

Storms

9

6.5

Storms River Route

Blue Lilies Bush

3.5

Dolphin Trail

Storms River Mouth

Storms River Beach

Mosterd se Krans

Grootbaai

INDIAN OCEAN

Plaatbos Nature Reserve

ELEVATION ABOVE SEA LEVEL (METRES)

| 75 | 150 | 225 | 300 | 375 | 450 | 525 | 600 | 675 | 750 | 825 | 900 | 975 | 1050 | 1125 | 1200 | 1275 | 1350 | 1425 | 1500 | 1575 |

127

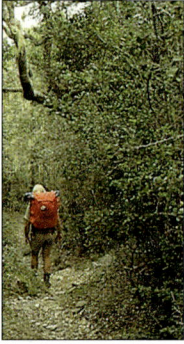

THINGS TO DO, PLACES TO VISIT

The activity grids on these pages have been designed in conjunction with the maps on pages 120 - 127. Each grid is coded with different bands of colour relating respectively to Maps 1 - 4.

The entries on the grids appear in order of their geographical position on the map, reading from left to right. Whatever magic you are hoping to discover along the Garden Route, these activity grids will help you to access the best that the area has to offer.

KEY TO MAP COLOURS

Map 1
(pages 120 - 121)

Map 2
(pages 122 - 123)

Map 3
(pages 124 - 125)

Map 4
(pages 126 - 127)

CONTENTS

KEY TO AUTHORITIES

ABM	–	Albertinia Municipality
DWAF	–	Dept. of Water Affairs and Forestry
GBM	–	Great Brak Municipality
GM	–	George Municipality
KM	–	Knysna Municipality
LM	–	Langerberg Municipality
MBM	–	Mossel Bay Municipality
MBP	–	Mossel Bay Port
NV	–	Nature's Valley
P	–	Private
PBM	–	Plettenberg Bay Municipality
SAF	–	SAFCOL
SANP	–	South African National Parks
SBM	–	Still Bay Municipality
SM	–	Sedgefield Municipality
WCNCB	–	Western Cape Nature Conservation Board
WM	–	Wilderness Municipality
WT	–	Wilderness Tourism

CAR RENTALS

LOCATION		TEL. NO.
Budget:		
George	town	044 – 873 6259
	airport	044 – 876 9204
		044 – 876 9216
Plettenberg Bay		044 – 533 2197
Avis:		
George	airport	044 – 876 9314
Plettenberg Bay		044 – 533 1315
Imperial:		
George		044 – 876 9017
Plettenberg Bay		044 – 533 3176

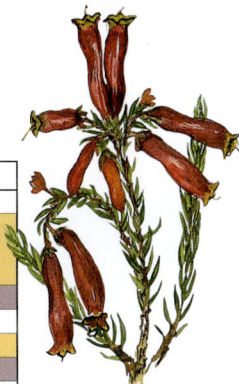

Erica versicolor (page 66) is one of the special fynbos plants.

INFORMATION CENTRES

LOCATION	TEL. NO.
Cape Town Routes Unlimited	021 – 487 4800
South African National Parks	021 – 426 4260
Still Bay	028 – 754 2602
Mossel Bay Tourism	044 – 691 2202
Great Brak Museum & Tourism	044 – 620 3338
George Tourism	044 – 801 9295
Wilderness Tourism	044 – 877 0045
Sedgefield	044 – 343 2658
Knysna	044 – 382 5510
Plettenberg Bay	044 – 533 4065
	044 – 533 3732
Bloukrans Bridge	042 – 281 1450
Storms River	042 – 280 3561

DISTANCE GRID

This table summarises the distances and travelling times between major centres, driving along tar roads only. Travelling times are estimated at an average of 100 km/hr.

TOWNS	DISTANCE	TIME
Still Bay to Gouritsmond	109 km	1 hour 10 min
Still Bay to Mossel Bay	113 km	1 hour 25 min
Gouritsmond to Mossel Bay	80 km	1 hour
Mossel Bay to George	45 km	30 minutes
Mossel Bay to Wilderness	54 km	40 minutes
George to Wilderness	16 km	15 minutes
Wilderness to Sedgefield	22 km	15 minutes
Sedgefield to Knysna	36 km	25 minutes
Knysna to Plettenberg Bay	32 km	25 minutes
Plettenberg Bay to Natures Valley	37 km	30 minutes
Plettenberg Bay to Storms River	74 km	45 minutes
Nature's Valley to Storms River	45 km	30 minutes

AIRLINES SERVICING THE GARDEN ROUTE

LOCATION	TEL. NO.
Sabena-Nationwide:	
George	044 – 801 8412
SA Airlink:	
George	044 – 801 8410
Plettenberg Bay	044 – 533 9041
SAA:	
George	044 – 801 8448

Fynbos in full colour

The Cape Sugarbird (page 98) is an endemic bird to fynbos and the area.

CARAVAN SITES

LOCATION	TEL. NO.	Restaurant/Kiosk	Swimming Pool / Tidal Pool	AUTH
Jongersfontein	028 – 755 8015			LM
Riverside	028 – 754 1608	•		P
Ellensrus	028 – 754 1034			SBM
Dias Beach	–	•	•	P
De Bakke/Santos Caravan Park	044 – 691 2915			MBM
Die Punt Caravan Park	044 – 690 3501	•	•	MBM
Glentana	044 – 879 1536			P
George Tourist Resort	044 – 874 5205	•		P
Ebb and Flow (Wilderness)	044 – 877 1197	•		WM
Woodbourne (Knysna)	044 – 384 0316			P
Monks (Knysna)	044 – 382 2609	•		P
Lake Brenton (Knysna)	044 – 381 0060	•		P
Keurbooms Lagoon (Plett)	044 – 533 2567			P
San Marino Holiday Resort	044 – 535 9700	•		P
Aventura Eco Plettenberg	044 – 535 9309	•		P
Dune Park Holiday Resorts	044 – 535 9606	•	•	P
Arch Rock	044 – 535 9409			P
Lily Pond (The Crags)	044 – 534 8767	•		NV
Storms River Mouth	042 – 281 1607		•	SANP

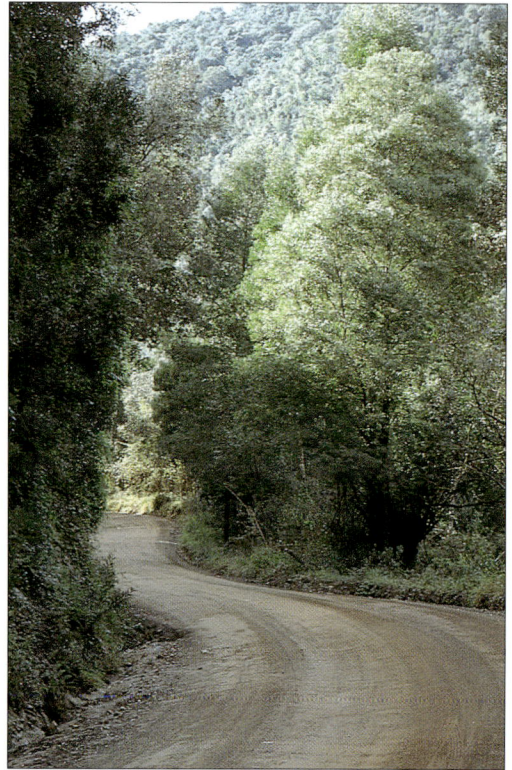

A forested drive between Knysna and George

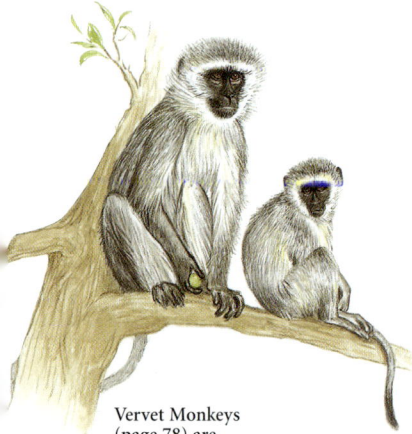

Vervet Monkeys (page 78) are occasionally spotted along the roadside and at caravan parks, in forested areas. Please do not feed these or any other wild animals.

SCENIC ROUTES AND DRIVES

The entire Garden Route is scenic, however we have listed below the most spectacular short or day trips. Refer to the maps (pages 120 - 127) for distances. * Indicates picnic spots.

NAME/ROUTE	COMMENTS
The Outeniqua Choo-tjoe, George to Knysna	Relaxing coastal route by steam train Tel.no. 044-801-8288 / 8264 / 8289 / 8202
Still Bay to Gourits River Mouth	Unusual coastline, exquisite fynbos, old architecture
*The Outeniqua Pass, Oudtshoorn to George	Spectacular mountain views, built 1943-1951
*The Montagu Pass, Oudtshoorn to George	Original ox-wagon pass, built 1844-1848
*The Seven Passes, George to Knysna	Mountain, country and indigenous forests
*The Old Cape Road to Kom se Pad, Knysna	Mountain and indigenous forests
*R339: Prince Alfred's Pass, Knysna to Diepwalle	Indigenous forests, good view spot at Spitskop, 933 m high
Stinkhout Draai, 2 km east of Garden of Eden	Indigenous forest drive
*Harkerville to Kranshoek, Plettenberg Bay	Indigenous forests, coastal view spot
*R340: Plettenberg Bay to Kruisvallei	Excellent vantage point to view the Tsitsikamma and Wynandskraal Mnts.
*R102: Grootrivier Pass, Nature's Valley	Indigenous forests, valleys and sightings of ancient yellowwood trees.
*Marine Drive, Turn off R102 at Bloukrans Forestry Station	Circular drive, panoramic views of Storms River to Plettenberg Bay and Formosa Peak
*R102: Bloukrans Pass	Indigenous forests and valleys

TOURS

ECO-ADVENTURE

NAME/LOCATION	TEL. NO.	AUTH.
Eco Bound	044 – 871 4455	P
Outeniqua Adventure Tours	044 – 871 1470	P
Eden Adventures	044 – 877 0179	P
Eco-Afrika Tours	044 – 384 0479	P
Knysna Elephant Park	044 – 532 7732	P
Monkeyland	044 – 534 8906	P
Storms River Adventures	042 – 281 1836	P

Treetop Canopy Tours; Black-water tubing; Gorge Challenge (abseiling, tubing, mountain biking); Boat cruises; Kouga Bush Camp (abseiling, rafting, team building); Woodcutters Journey; Mountain bike trails; Marine & Agricultural Tours

CULTURAL

NAME/LOCATION	TEL. NO.	COMMENTS
George – Khulani Xhosa Village	044 – 874 4401 083 630 6917	Traditional Xhosa crafts & culture, singing, dancing; other rituals
Knysna Heads Adventures	044 –384 0831	Township Trail Tour; Sangoma; Xhosa dancing

SELF-GUIDED

NAME/LOCATION	TEL. NO.	COMMENTS
George – Outeniqua Country Hop	044 – 870 0960	Garden Route's self-guided tourist route – arts and crafts; strawberry picking; outdoor activities; bird farm; animal farm

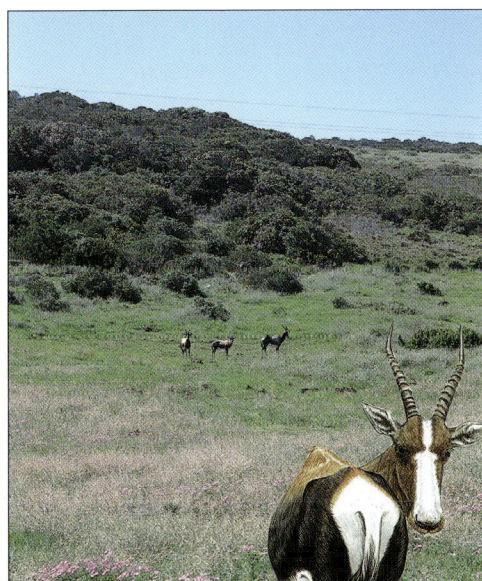

Rein's Coastal Nature Reserve

Bontebok (page 79)

The entries on the grids appear in order of their geographical position on the map, reading from left to right.

EASY-TO-ACCESS INDIGENOUS VEGETATION

These places can be visited either by car, or by a short, easy walk. A beautiful gum-tree plantation and information display at Bracken Hill Falls is worth visiting.

LOCATION	Dune Vegetation	Estuary	Forest	Fynbos
Geelkrans Nature Reserve				•
Rein's Coastal Nature Reserve				•
Ballots Bay			•	
Seven Passes			•	•
Pledge Nature Reserve				•
R339 to Knoetze			•	•
Kranshoek			•	•
Robberg Gate Car Park				•
R340 (Wittedrift - Kruisvalley)				•
Heidehof (The Crags)				•
R102 (Off N2 Natures Valley - Road to Platbank No 3)	•			•
Nature's Valley Town				•
Tsitsikamma Lodge			•	•
N2 Tollgate (Stormsriver)			•	
Garden of Eden			•	
Aventura Eco Plettenberg Holiday Resort			•	
Forest Hall				•
Goosemarsh		•		

PARKS, RESERVES AND GAME FARMS

There are a number of conserved areas along the Garden Route. See pages 78 - 79 for more information on land mammals.

*Indicates the presence of the larger mammals.

LOCATION	TEL. NO.	AUTH.
Pauline Bohnen Nature Reserve	028 – 754 2602	SBM
*Rein's Coastal Nature Reserve	028 – 745 3322	P
Imbabala Game Farm	044 – 695 2767	P
Zingela Indlela Game Tracks	044 – 694 0011	P
*Botlierskop Game Farm	044 696 6055	P
Outeniqua Nature Reserve	044 – 870 8323	WCNCB
Ballots Bay Nature Reserve	044 – 880 1153	P
Wilderness National Park	044 – 877 0046	SANP
Goukamma Nature Reserve	044 – 383 0042	WCNCB
Featherbed Nature Reserve	044 – 382 1693	P
Sinclair Nature Reserve	044 – 302 5600	DWAF
Ysterhout Rug	044 – 382 5466	DWAF
*Robberg Nature Reserve	044 – 533 2125	WCNCB
Keurbooms Nature Reserve	044 – 533 2125	WCNCB
Hog Hollow	044 – 534 8769	P
Monkeyland	044 – 534 8906	P
Lily Pond	044 – 534 8767	P
Tsitsikamma National Park	042 – 281 1607	SANP
Plaatbos Nature Reserve	042 – 281 1557	DWAF

BIRDING

The Garden Route is famous for its birds. The listed places tend to be most rewarding, and are easily accessible. See pages 94 - 105 for more information.

Binoculars and field note book are handy for recording observations.

LOCATION	Coastal	Forest	Fynbos	Estuary/Inland Water	Mountain	River	AUTH
Pauline Bohnen Nature Reserve	•		•				P
Geelkrans Walk	•		•				WCNCB
Rein's Coastal Nature Reserve	•		•				P
Elbertsvlei				•			P
Voëlvlei				•			P
Gourits Mouth	•			•		•	M
Seal Island	•						PT
Haartebeeskuil Dam				•			MBP
Geelbekvlei				•			MBP
Little Brak Estuary	•			•		•	MBP
Garden Route Dam		•			•	•	GM
Ballots Bay	•	•	•			•	P
Groeneweide Forest Walk		•			•	•	DWAF
Outeniqua Hiking trail		•	•		•	•	DWAF
Kingfisher Trails	•	•	•	•		•	SANP
Cape Dune Molerat			•			•	SANP
Langvlei Hide		•				•	SANP
Rondevlei Hide		•				•	SANP
Willow Point	•					•	SANP
Groenvlei			•	•			WCNCB
Goukamma Nature Reserve	•		•		•	•	WCNCB
Buffalo Valley Game Farm	•		•				P
Belvidere Manor	•	•	•	•		•	P
Jubillee Creek Walk		•			•	•	DWAF
Lielievlei Nature Reserve		•	•			•	DWAF
Pledge Nature Reserve		•				•	KM
Featherbed Nature Reserve	•		•	•			P
Leisure Island	•						P
Woodbourne Pan	•			•		•	P
Knoetzie	•			•	•	•	DWAF
The Elephant Trails		•			•	•	DWAF
Garden of Eden		•					DWAF
Harkerville	•	•	•			•	DWAF
Wittedrift Nature Trails		•	•	•	•	•	PBM
Robberg Reserve	•		•		•		WCNCB
Aventura Eco Plettenberg		•			•	•	P
Piesang River	•			•	•	•	PBM
Bitou River	•			•		•	PBM
Keurbooms River Breeding Colony	•						WCNCB
Keurbooms Nature Reserve		•	•		•	•	WCNCB
De Vasselot Nature Reserve	•	•	•		•	•	SANP
Tsitsikamma National Park	•	•	•		•	•	SANP
Plaatbos Nature Reserve		•				•	DWAF

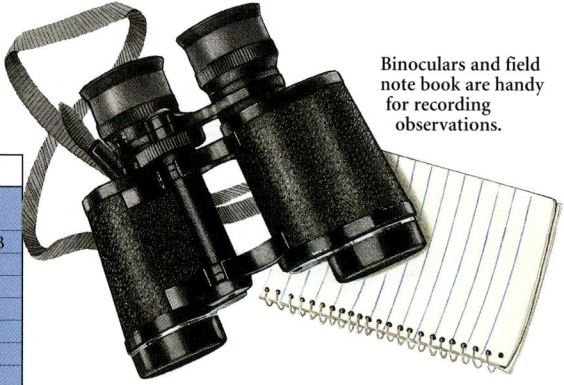

BIRD CLUBS

LOCATION	TEL. NO.
The Lakes Bird Club	044 – 871 2677
(Still Bay, Mossel Bay,	
George, Wilderness,	
Sedgefield, Knysna)	
Plettenberg Bay	-

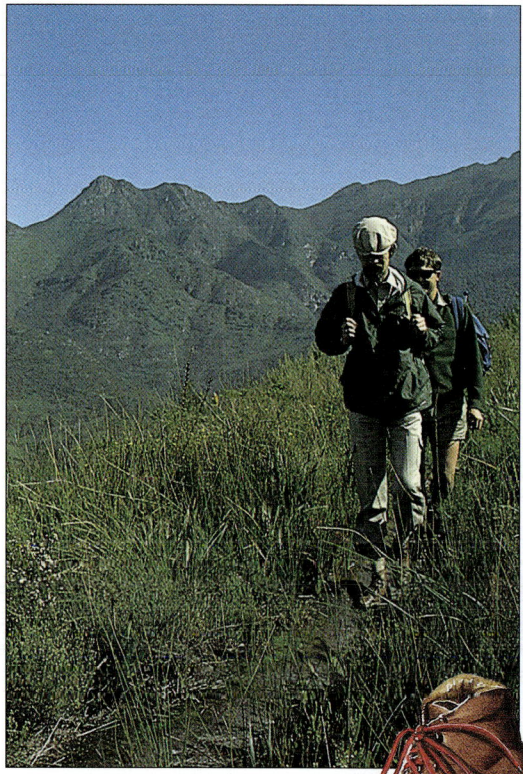

The Whimbrel (page 95) is one of many special water birds that can be viewed along the Garden Route.

The Garden Route is a hikers' and birders' paradise.

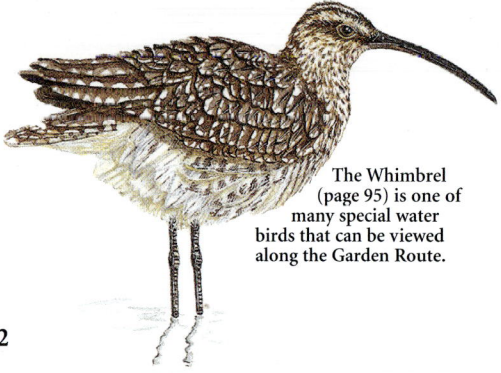

HIKING AND WALKING

The entire region is a paradise for hiking. The trails listed are the most accessible, well-marked and maintained. Please refer to the authority indicated for permits and information. SI = Self issued
* Indicates permits needed in school holidays only.

Key-hole limpets
(page 55)

LOCATION	TEL. NO.	DISTANCE	GRADING	PERMIT	Coastal	Forest	Fynbos	Estuary	River	Mountain	AUTH
Sleeping Beauty Trail	028 – 713 2418	13 km	Difficult	Yes	•	•	•			•	P
Crystal Kloof	028 –713 2418	21 km (2 days)	Easy	Yes		•	•				LM
Noordkapper Route	028 – 754 2602	11 km	Easy	No	•						SBM
Pauline Bohnen	028 – 754 2602	Differs	Varies	No			•				SBM
Strandloper Trail	028 – 754 2602	9 km	Easy	No			•				SBM
Wesoewer Trail	028 – 754 2602	3 km	Easy	No			•				SBM
Rein's Coastal Nature Reserve	028 – 745 3322	6 km	Easy	No	•		•				P
Cape St Blaize Trail	044 – 691 2202	15 km	Mod	No	•		•			•	MBM
Eight Bell Mountain Inn	044 – 631 0000	5 km	Varies	No		•	•	•			P
Glentana Beach Walk	044 – 801 9295	6 km	Easy	No	•						GM
Ghwano Bay to Rooikransies	044 – 873 6314	4 km	Easy	No	•						GM
Voëlklip to Herolds Bay	044 – 873 6314	4 km	Easy	No	•						GM
Herolds Bay to Scotts Bank	044 – 801 9295	4 km	Easy	No	•						GM
Duttons Cove Walk	044 – 801 9295	4km	Easy	No	•		•				GM
Cradock Pass Trail	044 – 870 8323	12 km	Difficult	SI		•				•	WCNCB
Pass to Pass Trail	044 – 870 8323	7 km	Varies	SI		•				•	WCNCB
Cradock/George Peak Trail	044 – 870 8323	18 km	Difficult	SI			•			•	WCNCB
Tierkop Hiking Trail	044 – 870 8323	14 km	Mod	Yes		•	•			•	WCNCB
Witfontein Forest Walks	044 – 870 8323	Varies	Easy	SI		•					WCNCB
Groeneweide Forest Walks	044 – 356 9021	Varies	Varies	SI		•					DWAF
Kingfisher Trails	044 – 877 1197	Varies	Varies	No		•			•	•	SANP
Cape Dune Molerat Trail	044 – 877 0045	8 km	Easy	No				•	•		SANP
Klein Krantz to Gerickes Point	044 – 877 0045	14 km	Easy	No	•						SANP
Swartvlei Beach Walk	044 – 877 0045	5 km	Mod	No	•						SANP
Outeniqua Trail	044 – 382 5466	108 km	Mod/Diff	Yes		•	•		•	•	DWAF
Attaquas Trail	044 – 870 8323	Differs	Difficult	Yes			•		•		WCNCB
Goukamma Beach Walk	044 – 343 2658	14 km	Easy	No	•						SM
*Jubilee Creek Walk	044 – 382 5466	4 km	Easy	No		•			•		DWAF
*Millwood Mine Walk	044 – 382 5466	5.6 km	Mod	*No		•	•				DWAF
Buffalo to Brenton Beach Walk	044 – 382 2095	7 km	Easy	No	•						WCNCB
*Terblans Walk	044 – 382 5466	7 km	Easy	*No		•					DWAF
*The Elephant Trails	044 – 382 5466	Differs	Varies	*No		•					DWAF
*Garden of Eden	044 – 382 5466	1 km	Easy	No		•					DWAF
Harkerville Coastal Trail	044 – 382 5466	26 km	Difficult	Yes	•	•	•		•		DWAF
Kranshoek Walk	044 – 382 5466	9 km	Mod/Diff	No	•	•	•				DWAF
Bracken Hill Waterfalls	044 – 375 0243	Differs	Varies	No		•			•		SAF
Wittedrift Nature Trails	044 – 533 2125	Differs	Easy/Diff	No		•			•		WCNCB
Robberg Guided Walks	044 – 533 2632	Differs	Varies	Yes	•	•	•			•	WCNCB
Robberg Natures Reserve	044 – 533 2125	Differs	Varies	Yes	•	•	•			•	WCNCB
Keurbooms – Matjies River Walk	044 – 533 3732	3 km	Mod	No					•		P
Keurbooms Forestry Station	044 – 534 8701	Differs	Easy	Yes		•					SAF
Nature Valley Trails (Refer to De Vasselot Camp Site for permit and maps)	044 – 531 6700	Differs	Varies	Yes	•	•	•	•	•	•	SANP
Tsitsikamma Hiking Trail	012 – 481 3615	61 km	Mod	Yes		•	•		•	•	SANP
Stinkhoutkloof Trail	042 – 291 0393	8,4 km	Difficult	SI		•			•		DWAF
Rugbos Trails	042 – 291 0393	Differs	Varies	SI		•	•		•	•	DWAF
Plaatbos Trails	042 – 291 0393	Differs	Mod	SI		•	•		•		DWAF
Otter Trail	012 – 428 9111	48 km	Difficult	Yes	•	•	•		•	•	SANP
Dolphin Trail	042 – 280 3818	20 km	Easy/Mod	Yes	•						SANP
Storms River Mouth Trails (Refer to Storms River Mouth office for permits and maps)	042 – 281 1607	Differs	Varies	No	•	•	•		•		SANP

A good pair of hiking boots or walking shoes is advised.

HISTORICAL SITES

Read about the human history on pages 104 - 113.
The numbers next to each location appear on the maps.
The following themes are marked:

EH = Early History, pages 104 - 107
TES = Travellers & Early Settlers, pages 108 - 109
NTC = Nineteenth & Twentieth Centuries, pages 110 - 113

* These references appear on the maps but not in the text although they relate to the period/theme.

NO. ON MAP	LOCATION	HISTORY PAGE REF.	THEME
1	Fish Traps	107	EH
2	*Pallinggat Homestead	110	NTC
3	*Melkhoutfontein	108	TES
4	Rein's Nature Reserve Gouriqua	104	EH
5	*St Blaize Lighthouse	108	TES
6	*Bats Cave	106	EH
7	Cape St Blaize Cave	106	EH
8	Bartolomeu Diaz Centre	108	TES
9	Post Office Tree	109	TES
10	*Historical Walk	110	NTC
11	*Floating Dock Wreck, 2 km east Glentana	108	TES
12	*Walking Tour, George	110	NTC
13	*Tree & Timber Museum	108	TES
14	*Pacaltsdorp Stone Church Captain Dikkop's Grave 2-roomed cottage Patat Huisie	108	TES
15	*Seven Passes Road	108	TES
16	*Ebb and Flow Cave, near Wilderness	104	EH
17	*Portland Manor Estate	110	NTC
18	*Millwood Goldmine Ruins	113	NTC
19	Belvidere Church	111	NTC
20	*Town Walking Tour Knysna	110	NTC
21	*Yacht Club Early Landing Sites	108	TES
22	Outeniqua Railroad/Chootjoe	113	NTC
23	*Paquila Wreck	108	TES
24	*Strandloper Cave 1	104	EH
25	*The Bar & Pilot Station	110	NTC
26	George Rex Grave Site	111	NTC
27	*La Fleur Graves	108	TES
28	*St Andrew's Church	108	TES
29	*Weldon House (orig. Plett Post Office)	110	NTC
30	*Athena Wreck	110	NTC
31	Nelson Bay Cave	105	EH
32	Old Whaling Station Site	113	NTC
33	*Navigational Beacon	108	TES
34	*Old Timber Store Ruins	108	TES
35	*Old Rectory	108	TES
36	Van Plettenberg Stone	109	TES
37	*St Peter's Church	108	TES
38	*Jerling Collection	108	TES
39	Matjies River Rock Shelter	106	EH
40	*Forest Hall	110	NTC
41	*De Vasselot Camp Site	110	NTC
42	*Bloukrans Pass	108	TES
43	*Big Tree	104	EH
44	*Strandloper Cave 2	104	EH
45	*Storms River Pass	108	TES

An early
navigational
instrument
(page 108)

HISTORICAL INFORMATION

All places of interest are listed and marked on the maps.
For further information refer to the following instructions.

LOCATION	INSTITUTION	TEL. NO.
Still Bay	Publicity	028 – 754 2602
Mossel Bay	Bartolomeu Dias Museum	044 – 691 1067
George	Museum	044 – 873 5343
Knysna	Angling Club	044 – 382 4002
Knysna	Library	044 – 302 6300
Knysna	Millwood Museum	044 – 302 6300
Plettenberg Bay	Central Library	044 – 501 3130

ARTS AND CRAFTS

LOCATION	TEL. NO.
The Model Shipyard	044 – 691 1531
Strydom Gallery	044 – 874 4027
Scarab Paper	044 – 343 2455
Candlepower	044 – 343 1097
Hot Art	044 – 343 1123
Bitou-on-the-Water and Bitou Crafts	044 – 382 3251
Crazy Clay	044 – 382 5394
The Potter	044 – 532 7735
The Heath Store	044 – 532 7724
Elephant Walk Stall	044 – 532 7833
Weldon Kaya Crafts	044 – 533 2437
Global Village	044 – 533 5150
Earth Sea Creations	082 378 8060
Old Nick Pottery & Weaving	044 – 533 1395
Porcupine Ceramic Arts	044 – 534 8910

The Information Centre at Still Bay is housed in
a national monument.

GOLF COURSES

Each golf course has its own specific regulations. Please enquire at each club for details.

LOCATION	TEL. NO.
Still Bay Golf Club	028 – 754 2625
Mossel Bay	044 – 691 2379
Fancourt	044 – 804 0000
George Golf Club	044 – 873 6116
Knysna	044 – 384 1150
Sparrebosch Golf Club	044 – 384 1104
Plettenberg Bay Country Club	044 – 533 2132
Goose Valley	044 – 533 5082

Fancourt Golf Course in George

HORSE AND PONY RIDING

Various stables and riding schools offer day 'outrides' into the wilderness areas and forests, and onto the beaches.

Horse riding stirrup

STABLE	TEL. NO.	RIDES
George Riding Centre	044 – 871 3256	Various
Forest Horse Rides/Knysna	044 – 388 4764	Various
Harkerville Horse Rides	044 – 532 7777	Various
Equatrailing/Plettenberg Bay	044 – 533 0599	Various
Southern Comfort Horse Trails/Plettenberg Bay	044 – 532 7885	Various
Fourfields Horses (The Crags)	044 - 53 48708	Various

DRIVING RANGES

LOCATION	TEL. NO.
Mossel Bay	044 – 691 2379
George: Vodacom Golf Village	044 – 871 4001

CYCLING

Most of the popular routes have been marked on the map. Some are not designated trails, but are ideal for cycling. Refer to relevant publicity offices for more information.

ROUTE	TEL. NO.	DISTANCE	GRADING	Coastal	Forest	Fynbos	Estuary	River	Mountain	AUTH
Still Bay Bike Trail	028 – 754 2602	Differs	Easy	•		•				SBM
Rein's Coastal Nature Reserve	028 – 745 3322	Differs	Easy	•		•		•		P
Rein's Coastal Nature Reserve to Gourits Mouth	028 – 745 3322	25 km	Varies	•						P
Geelhoutboom Trail/George	044 – 801 9295	18 km	Easy		•		•		•	GM
Outeniqua Adventure Tours/George (Little Karoo and Garden Route)	044 – 871 1470	2 – 6 days	Varies	•	•	•	•	•	•	P
Montagu Pass Bike Trail/George	044 – 801 9295	12 km	Varies		•	•			•	GM
Garden Route Dam/George	044 – 801 9295	3 km	Easy		•					GM
The Vlei Sand Road/ Wilderness	044 – 877 0045	18 km	Easy	•						WT
The 7 Passes Rd/Wilderness to Knysna	044 – 871 4455	57 km	Varies		•	•			•	GM
Homtini Cycle Route/Knysna	044 – 382 5466	19 km	Varies		•			•		DWAF
Petrus se Brand/Diepwalle to Harkerville	044 – 382 5466	24 km	Varies		•				•	DWAF
Harkerville Cycle Routes	044 – 877 0577	Differs	Varies		•					DWAF
Outeniqua Biking Trails/Plettenberg Bay	044 – 532 7644	Differs	Varies	•	•	•			•	DWAF
Wittedrift Nature Trail/Plettenberg Bay	044 – 533 4065	Differs	Easy		•		•		•	PBM
Prince Alfred Pass	044 – 533 4065	Differs	Varies			•			•	PBM
Robbehoek Cycling Route	083 261 4826	Differs	Varies	•	•	•			•	P
Tsitsikamma National Park/Storms River	042 – 281 1607	Differs	Easy		•	•				SANP
Storms River Adventures	042 – 281 1815/36	Differs	Varies	•	•	•		•		P

BEACHES

Water temperatures vary from 14º to 23º, depending on seasons and weather conditions. Lifeguards are generally on duty only in December and January, and in the April school holidays.

The entries on the grids appear in order of their geographical position on the map, reading from left to right.

LOCATION	Toilets & Showers	Restaurant	Braai facilities	Shop/Kiosk	Lifeguards	Body boarding/Surfing	Tidal Pool	AUTH
Jongensfontein	•		•		•		•	SBM
Shelly								SBM
Lappies Bay	•	•		•		•		SBM
Gourits	•						•	SBM
Cannon								MBP
Vleesbaai						•		MBP
Santos	•	•		•		•		MBP
Dias	•			•		•		MBP
Hartenbos	•	•		•		•		MBP
Little Brak	•			•		•		MBP
Tergniet	•							MBP
Great Brak								GBM
Glentana	•	•		•		•	•	GM
Herolds Bay	•		•		•		•	GM
Victoria Bay	•	•	•	•		•	•	GM
Wilderness	•		•	•		•		SANP
Wilderness Dune						•		SANP
Klein Krantz	•					•		SANP
Swartvlei	•			•		•		SANP
Myoli	•					•		SM
Sedgefield	•			•		•		SM
Goukamma								WCNCB
Buffalo Bay	•	•		•		•	•	WCNCB
Brenton	•	•		•		•		KM
Coney Glen	•					•		KM
Knoetzie								KM
Island								WCNCB
Robberg Corner						•		WCNCB
Robberg 5	•			•		•		PBM
Robberg Beacon Island	•					•		PBM
Central	•	•	•	•		•		PBM
Hobie	•					•		PBM
The Wedge						•		PBM
Lookout	•	•		•		•		PBM
Keurbooms	•			•		•		WCNCB
Cathedral Rock								WCNCB
Salt River Mouth								WCNCB
Nature's Valley	•			•		•		SANP
Storms River	•	•	•	•	•	•		SANP

Southern Right Whale (page 38), the most commonly sighted whales off the Garden Route coast

SCUBA DIVING AND SNORKELLING

Diving and snorkelling along the Garden Route are excellent. Contact the numbers below for further information, hire of equipment and tuition.

LOCATION	TEL. NO.
Mossel Bay Diving Academy	082 896 5649
Beyond the Beach, Plettenberg Bay	044 – 533 1158
Ocean Safaris, Plettenberg Bay	044 – 533 4963
Storms River Adventures	042 – 281 1836

DEEP SEA SAFARIS

NAME/LOCATION	TEL NO.
Romonza – Mossel Bay (June – Oct)	044 – 690 3101
Deep sea fishing with Go Fish	084 626 3190 072 255 5313
Ocean Blue Adventures – Plettenberg Bay	044 – 533 5083
Ocean Safaris – Plettenberg Bay	044 – 533 4963
The Explorer Adventures – Plettenberg Bay	044 – 533 5241

WHALE WATCHING

Land-based whale watching is at its best from July to October. See pages 38 - 40 for more information.

LOCATION	AUTH
Die Poort	MBP
Fransmanhoek	MBP
Gourits Mouth	ABM
Great Brak River	GBM
Jongensfontein	SBM
Lappies Bay	SBM
Morris Point	SBM
Rein's Coastal Nature Reserve	P
Ballots Bay	P
Cape Windlass	GM
Dolphin Point	GM
Herolds Bay	GM
Lands End Guest House	GM
Platbank No 1	WCNCB
The Waves B&B	P
Wilderness Dune Beach	GM
Brenton-on-Sea	P
Knoetzie	KM
Kranshoek Viewsite	P
The Heads	KM
Walker Point	SANP
Keurbooms Hill	P
Nature's Valley	SANP
Robberg Nature Reserve	WCNCB
Signal Hill	PBM
Storms River Mouth	SANP

Kelp Gulls
(page 90),
a common sea
bird in the area

National Sea Rescue Institute

SEA RESCUE

The NSRI operates all along the Garden Route coast offering emergency life-saving services with their fleet of volunteer-manned Sea Rescue crew. These services required substantial donations.

LOCATION	EMERGENCY TEL. NO.	
Mossel Bay	044 – 10177	(Ambulance service)
	044 – 691 1911	(Ambulance service)
Wilderness	044 – 873 3343	(NSRI)
Knysna	044 – 384 0211 / 082 990 5956	
	044 – 302 6600	(Police)
Plettenberg Bay	10111	(Flying Squad)
	044 – 533 2744	(NSRI)

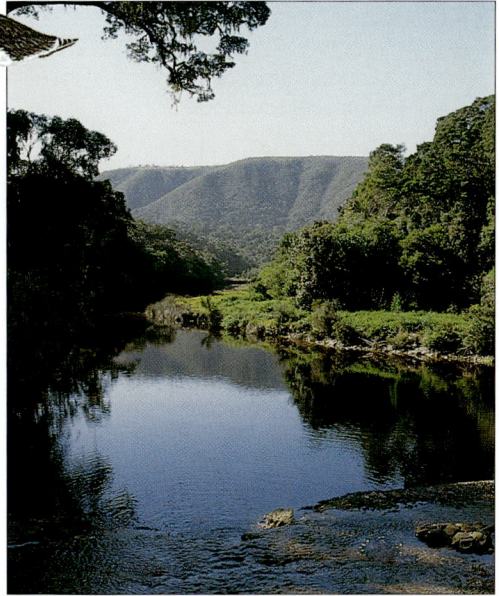
Groot River at Nature's Valley, a peaceful spot to picnic and swim

FRESH WATER SWIMMING

Swimming areas other than in the sea are listed below.

LOCATION	TEL. NO.	River	Lagoon/Estuary	Municipal Pool	AUTH
Still Bay	028 – 754 2602	•	•		SBM
Little Brak	044 – 691 2202	•	•	•	MBM
Great Brak	044 – 620 2100	•		•	GBM
Wilderness/Island Lake	044 – 877 0046	•	•		SANP
Swartvlei	044 – 877 1197		•	•	SANP
Groenvlei Lake	044 – 383 0042		•		WCNCB
Goukamma	044 – 383 0042				WCNCB
Plettenberg Bay	044 – 533 4065		•		PBM
Plettenberg Bay/Keurbooms River and Lagoon	044 – 533 2125	•	•		WCNCB
Nature's Valley/Groot River Lagoon	044 – 531 6835		•		SANP

Giant Kingfisher
(page 92)
is a common
freshwater
bird.

Robberg, at Plettenberg Bay is a beautiful beach and a good place to sight whales and dolphins.

ANGLING

Many fish are threatened in the area. Make sure you know the local rules before setting out. See fish species on pages 44 - 49.

*Indicates freshwater angling spots

LOCATION	AUTH
Voëlklip	SBM
Masterstock	SBM
Lappies Bay Beach	SBM
Preekstoel	SBM
Rooibankies	MBM
Fransmanshoek	MBM
Vleespunt	MBM
Pinnacle Point	MBM
Die Poort	MBM
Romansbank Rocks	MBM
Harbour Wall Mossel Bay	MBM
Die Bakke	MBM
Hartenbos Beach	MBM
*Great Brak Estuary/River	GBM
Cape Windlass	GM
Rooikransies	GM
Voëlklip	GM
Scotts Bank	GM
Preekstoel	GM
Jacobs Point	GM
Rooiklip	GM
Victoria Bay	GM
Leentjiesklip	GM
Flat Rock	GM
Gerickes Point	SANP
*Swartvlei Lake/Estuary/Lagoon	SANP
Groenvlei	WCNCB
Goukamma Beach	WCNCB
Platbank No 1	PBM
Goukamma River Mouth	WCNCB
Rowwehoek	WCNCB
Walker Point	WCNCB
Castle Rock	KM
*Knysna Lagoon	KM
Coney Glen Beach	KM
Knoetzie	KM
Stevens Bank	PBM
Stilbaai	PBM
Platbank No 2	PBM
The Island	PBM
The Ledge	PBM
Kanon Koël Gat	PBM
Meide Bank	PBM
Beacon Island Rocks	PBM
Lookout Rocks	PBM
*Keurbooms Lagoon	WCNCB
Aventura Eco Plettenberg	P
Keurbooms Beach	PBM
Picnic Rock	PBM
Grootbank	PBM
Blue Rocks	PBM

Sinkers used for fishing

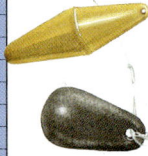

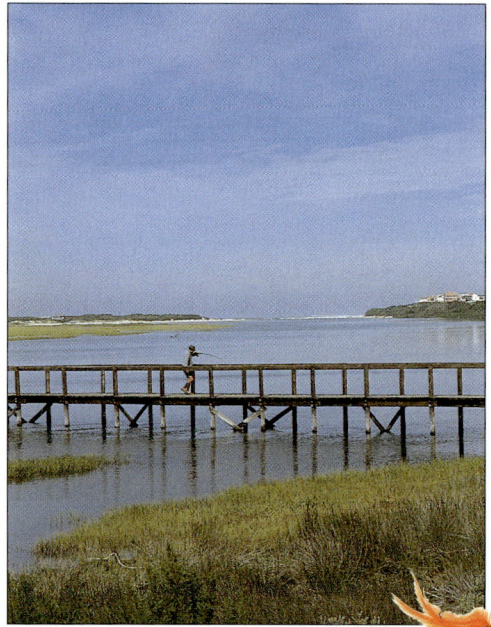

Angling at Still Bay estuary

Flyfishing fly

Fishing swivels

Mossel Bay harbour, from where one can fish or launch a sail boat

ANGLING CLUBS & INFORMATION CENTRES

All well-known fishing spots are listed and marked on the maps.

LOCATION	TEL. NO.
Still Bay	028 – 754 2602
Mossel Bay	044 – 690 7100
George (Mr Lammers)	044 – 889 0167
George Bass Club (Freshwater)	044 – 875 9197
Knysna	044 – 382 4002
Plettenberg Bay	044 – 535 9740

Fishing rod and hooks

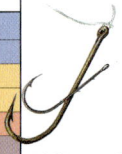

138

CANOEING / KAYAKING

LOCATION	TEL. NO.	HIRE	AUTH
Eden Adventures Garden Route Dam	044 – 877 0179		GM
Ebb and Flow/ Wilderness	044 – 877 1197		SANP
Fairy Knowe Hotel/Wilderness	044 – 877 1100	•	P
Eden Adventures/Wilderness	044 – 877 0179		P
Lake Pleasant/Sedgefield	044 – 383 1985	•	P
Groenvlei	044 – 383 0042		WCNCB
Goukamma Nature Reserve	044 – 383 0042		WCNCB
Dolphin Adventures	044 – 384 1536		P
Knysna Eco-Ventures	044 – 382 5920		P
Knysna Lagoon	044 – 382 2905		SANP
Real Cape Adventures	082 – 556 2520		P
	021 – 790 5611		
Ocean Safaris Plettenberg Bay	044 – 533 4963	•	P
Aventura Eco Plettenberg Bay	044 – 535 9309		P
Keurbooms River	044 – 533 2125	•	WCNCB
Nature's Valley Lagoon	044 – 531 6835		SANP

Sailing
boat ropes

Red Roman,
page 47

SAILING

Designated areas have specific regulations. Refer to authorities listed below. Hire and charter vessels and tuition are available.

*Indicates freshwater sailing

LOCATION	TEL. NO.	AUTH
Mossel Bay Harbour	044 – 604 6271	MBM
George / Garden Route Dam (canoes only)	044 – 801 9295 (Tourism office)	GM
*Island Lake/Wilderness	044 – 877 0046	SANP
*Swartvlei Lake/Sedgefield	044 – 877 0046	SANP
Baywater Village	044 – 343 2008	P
*Groenvlei/Sedgefield	044 – 383 0042	WCNCB
Buffalo Bay/Knysna	044 – 382 5510	KM
*Knysna Lagoon	044 – 382 2095	SANP
Springtide Charters/Knysna	082 470 6022	P
Plettenberg Bay/Hobie Beach	044 – 533 2941	PSBC
*Nature's Valley Lagoon	044 – 531 6835	SANP
*Plettenberg Bay/Keurbooms Lagoon	044 – 533 2125	WCNCB

YACHT CLUBS

DESIGNATED AREAS	TEL. NO.	AUTH
Mossel Bay Yacht Club	044 – 690 7100	MBM
George Lakes Club	044 – 873 3656	P
Knysna Yacht Club	044 – 382 5724	P

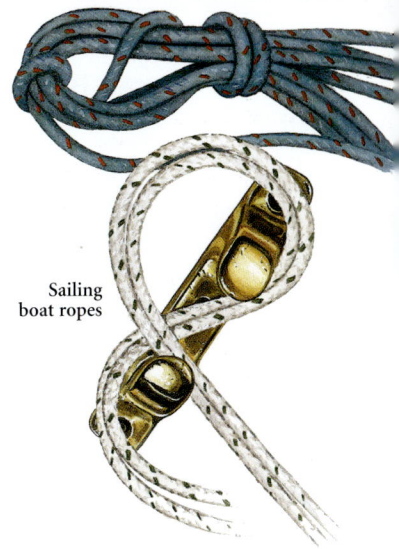

Swartvlei Lagoon

Spiny Starfish (page 50)

Heart Urchins
(page 76)

Take a boat cruise to Featherbed Reserve, on the western head of Knysna Heads.

BOAT CRUISES

*Indicates boats for hire as well

LOCATION	TEL. NO.	AUTH
Romonza/Mossel Bay	044 – 690 3101	P
Seven Seas/Mossel Bay	044 – 691 3371	P
John Benn/Featherbed Reserve Knysna	044 – 382 1693	P
Knysna Waterfront Ferries	044 – 382 5520	P
*Aventura Eco Plettenberg Bay (private except peak time Dec/Jan)	044 – 535 9309	P
Ocean Adventures/ Plettenberg Bay	044 – 533 5083	P
Stanley Island/Plettenberg Bay	044 – 535 9442	P
Dave Rissik	044 – 533 5083	P
Storms River Cruises/ Tsitsikamma Nature Reserve	042 – 281 1815/36	P

WATER SKIING

This sport is only allowed on water areas listed below. Please refer to relevant authorities for exact location.

DESIGNATED AREAS	TEL. NO.	AUTH
Great Brak River	044 – 620 2100	GBM
Sedgefield/ Swartvlei Lagoon/Lake	044 – 877 0046	SANP
Knysna Lagoon	044 – 382 2905	SANP
	044 – 382 5920	P
Plettenberg Bay/ Keurbooms River	044 – 533 2125	WCNCB
	044 – 533 3732	P

POWER BOATING

All boating requires permits. Boats may only be launched from designated launch sites. Ski boats must remain 300 m away from whales. Refer to authorities for rules and regulations.

*Indicates freshwater boating.

LAUNCH SITES	TEL. NO.	AUTH
Mossel Bay Harbour	044 – 604 6271	MBM
Great Brak River	044 – 620 2100	GBM
*Island Lake/Wilderness	044 – 877 1197	SANP
Sedgefield/ Swartvlei River Mouth	044 – 877 0046	SANP
Groenvlei Launch Site	044 – 383 0042	WCNCB
*Knysna Lagoon	044 – 382 2095	SANP
*Lake Brenton Resort	044 – 381 0060	P
Keurbooms River	044 – 533 2125	WCNCB
Plett Central Beach	044 – 533 2941	PSBC

SKI BOAT CLUBS

LOCATION	TEL. NO.	AUTH
Mossel Bay	044 – 690 7100	P
Plettenberg Bay	044 – 533 2941	PBM

The entries on the grids appear in order of their geographical position on the map, reading from left to right.

PARAGLIDING

LOCATION	TEL. NO.
Cloud Base/Wilderness	044 – 877 1414
	082 – 777 8474
Smile High/Knysna	044 – 384 0308

PARASAILING

COMPANY	TEL. NO.
Mossel Bay	083 – 303 1960
Ocean Safaris Plettenberg Bay	044 – 533 4963

BUNGEE/BRIDGE JUMPING

This sport is managed by Kiwi Extreme. They are a highly trained and professional crew and have two locations on the Garden Route.

LOCATION	TEL. NO.
Bloukrans River Bridge	042 – 281 1458
	216 m – World's Hightest!
	40 km east of Plettenberg Bay

ABSEILING

LOCATION	TEL. NO.
Storms River with Storms River Adventures	042 – 281 1815/36

AIR FLIPS

The following companies can be contacted for flips and trips.

LOCATION	TEL. NO.
Cape Flying Services/George	044 – 876 9217
African Ramble/Plettenberg Bay	044 – 533 9006
Ocean Safaris/Plettenberg Bay	044 – 533 4963
Stanley Island/Plettenberg Bay	044 – 535 9442

European Swallows and White-rumped Swifts in flight

Many inland areas are ideal for water recreation.

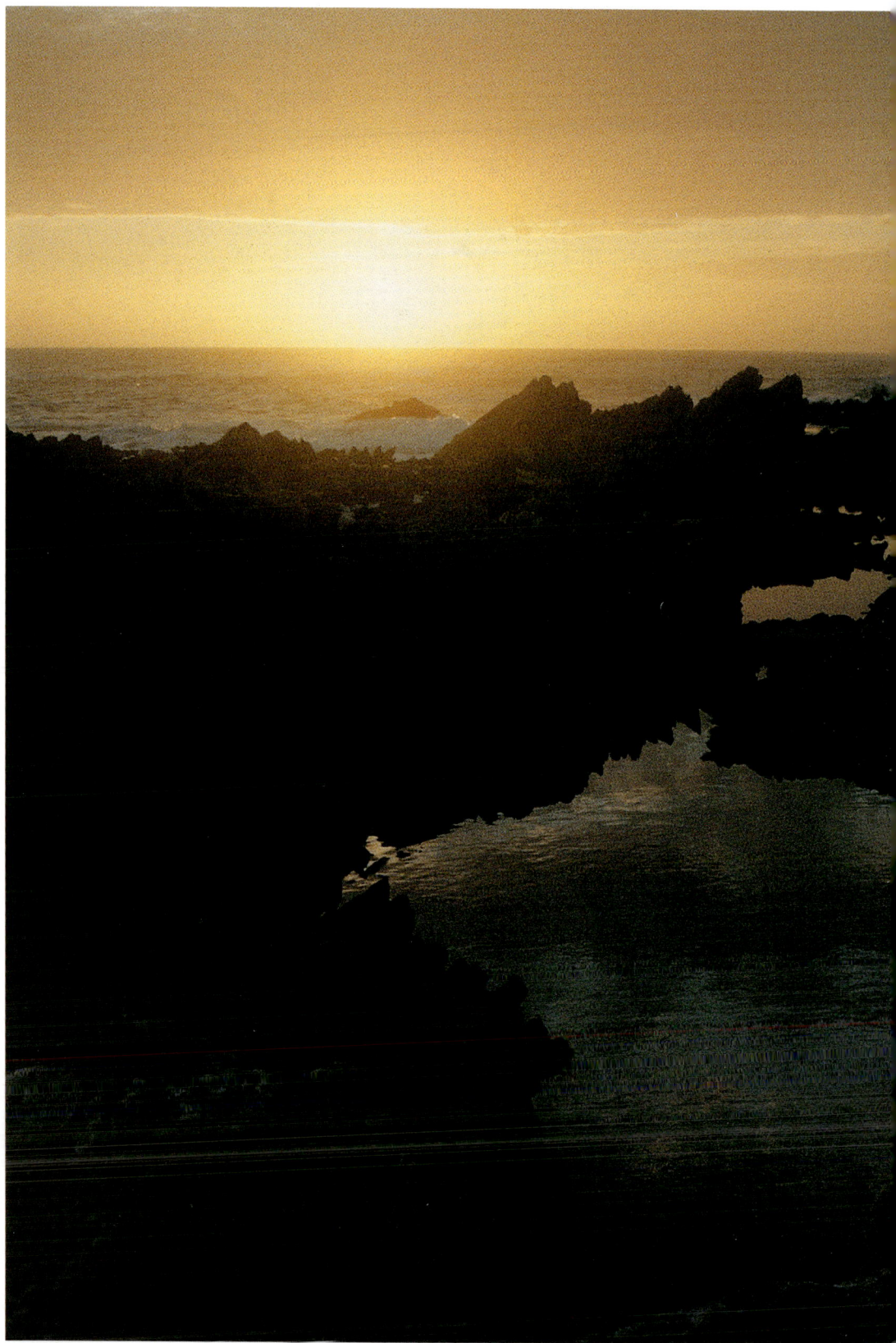

SUNSET SCENE

Nestling between mountain and sea, the natural beauty and wonder of the Garden Route lie waiting to be explored. This enticing stretch of coastline is a holiday-maker's paradise.

For outdoor enthusiasts there are endless opportunities and challenges. Many others return again and again simply to enjoy the uniquely beautiful scenery. They come to walk on soft, golden beaches, and to be rejuvenated by the Garden Route's special mixture of peace and tranquillity.

Leisurely travelling this short stretch of coastline, it would be impossible not to be captivated by its beauty and charm. As each bend in the road reveals new delights and uncovers new secrets, the Garden Route weaves its magic, welcoming one and all to the shining pearl of South Africa's coastline.

A striking sunset viewed from one of the many lookout points on the Otter Trail.

INDEX

144

*Striped Mouse,
page 80*

145

Erica
versicolor,
page 114

148

*Fiery-necked
Nightjar,
page 101*

149

NOTES